THE VIRGIN MARY IN THE KINGDOM OF THE DIVINE WILL

Meditations for the Month of May

Luisa Piccar

GW00535855

Content

3

Ecclesiastical seals of approval of the original Italian editions

First Edition (in Italian): + Imprimatur, the Episcopal Curia of Montepulciano, Italy, March 30, 1932

Second Edition (in Italian): + Nihil Obstat Quominus Reimprimatur, Joseph Blandamura, Delegate of the Archbishop of Taranto, Italy November 23, 1933

Third Edition (in Italian): + Nihil Obstat Quominus Reimprimatur, Msgr. Francis M. della Cueva S. M., Delegate of the Archbishop of Taranto, Italy (Feast of Christ the King) 1937

Ad usum privatum

Information: www.divinewill.eu

Maternal Appeal of the Queen of Heaven

Dearest child, I feel the irresistible need to descend from Heaven to make you my maternal visits. If you assure Me of your filial love and faithfulness, I will remain always with you in your soul, to be your teacher, model, example and most tender Mother.

I come to invite you to enter into the Kingdom of your Mother – that is, the Kingdom of the Divine Will; and I knock at the door of your heart, that you may open it to Me. You know? With my own hands I bring you this book as gift; I offer it to you with maternal care, so that, in your turn, in reading it, you may learn to live of Heaven and no longer of earth.

This book is of gold, my child. It will form your spiritual fortune, your happiness, also terrestrial. In it you will find the fount of all goods: if you are weak, you will acquire strength; if you are tempted, you will achieve victory; if you have fallen into sin, you will find the pitying and powerful hand that will lift you up again. If you feel afflicted, you will find comfort; if cold, the sure means to get warm; if hungry, you will enjoy the delicious food of the Divine Will. With it you will lack nothing; you will no longer be alone, because your Mother will keep you sweet company, and with Her every maternal care She will take on the commitment of making you happy. I, the Celestial Empress, will take care of all your needs, provided that you consent to live united with Me.

If you knew my yearnings, my ardent sighs, and also the tears I shed for my children...! If you knew how I burn with the desire that you listen to my lessons, all of Heaven, and learn to live of Divine Will...!

In this book you will see wonders; you will find a Mother who loves you so much as to sacrifice Her own beloved Son for you, in order to allow you to live of that same life of which She lived upon earth.

O please! do not give Me this sorrow - do not reject Me. Accept this gift of Heaven that I am bringing you; welcome my visit, my lessons. Know that I will go throughout the whole world; I will go to each individual, to all families, to religious communities, to every nation, to all peoples, and, if needed, I will go around for entire centuries until, as Queen, I have formed my people, and, as Mother, my children, who would know the Divine Will and let It reign everywhere.

Here is the purpose of this book explained to you. Those who will welcome it with love will be the first fortunate children who will belong to the Kingdom of the Divine Fiat; and I, with gold characters, will write their names in my maternal Heart.

See, my child, that same infinite love of God which, in Redemption, wanted to use Me in order to make the Eternal Word descend upon earth, is now calling Me into the field once again, entrusting to Me the difficult task, the sublime mandate of forming on earth the children of the Kingdom of His Divine Will. Therefore, with maternal care I set to work, and I prepare for you the way which will lead you to this happy Kingdom. For this purpose I will give you sublime and celestial lessons and, finally, I will teach you special and new prayers, through which you will commit the heavens, the sun, the Creation, my very life and that of my Son, and all the acts of the Saints, so that, in your name, they may impetrate the adorable Kingdom of the Divine Will. These prayers are the most powerful, because they bind the very divine operating. By means of them, God will feel disarmed and conquered by the creature. Confident of this help, you will hasten the coming of His most happy Kingdom, and, with Me, you will obtain that the Divine Will be done on earth as It is in Heaven, according to the desire of the Divine Master.

Courage, my child - make Me content, and I will bless you.

Prayer to the Celestial Queen for each day of the month of May

Immaculate Queen, my Celestial Mother, I come onto your maternal knees to abandon myself in your arms as your dear child, and to ask of You, with the most ardent sighs, in this month consecrated to You, the greatest of graces: that You admit me to live in the Kingdom of the Divine Will. Holy Mother, You who are the Queen of this Kingdom, admit me to live in It as your child, that It may no longer be deserted, but populated by your children. Therefore, Sovereign Queen, I entrust myself to You, that You may lead my steps in the Kingdom of the Divine Will; and as I cling to your maternal hand, You will lead all my being to live perennial life in the Divine Will. You will be my Mother, and to You, as my Mother, I deliver my will, that You may exchange it with the Divine Will, and so I may be sure I will not go out of Its Kingdom. Therefore I pray You to illumine me in order to make me comprehend what 'Will of God' means. *(Hail Mary)*

Little Sacrifice of the Month: Each morning, midday and night – three times a day – let us go onto the knees of our Celestial Mother, and say to Her: "My Mother, I love You; and You – love me, and give a sip of Divine Will to my soul. Give me your blessing, that I may do all of my actions under your maternal gaze.

Day One

The Queen of Heaven in the Kingdom of the Divine Will. The First Step of the Divine Will in the Immaculate Conception of the Celestial Mother.

The soul to her Immaculate Queen:

Here I am, O most sweet Mother, prostrate before You. Today is the first day of the month of May, consecrated to You, in which all your children want to offer You their little flowers to prove to You their love, and to bind your love to love them; and I see You as though descending from the Celestial Fatherland, attended by angelic cohorts, to receive the beautiful roses, the humble violets, the chaste lilies of your children, and requite them with your smiles of love, your graces and blessings. And pressing the gifts of your children to your maternal womb, You bring them with You to Heaven, to keep them as pledges and crowns for the moment of their death.

Celestial Mother, in the midst of many, I, who am the littlest, the neediest of your children, want to come up onto your maternal lap, to bring You, not flowers and roses, but a sun each day. But the Mother must help her child, giving me her lessons of Heaven, to teach me how to form these divine suns, that I may give You the most beautiful homage and the most pure love. Dear Mother, You have understood what your child wants: I want to be taught by You how to live of Divine Will. And I, transforming my acts and all of myself into Divine Will according to your teachings, each day, will bring You, onto your lap, all my acts changed into suns.

Lesson of the Queen of Heaven:

Blessed child, your prayer wounded my maternal Heart, and as it draws Me from Heaven, I am already close to my child, to give her my lessons, all of Heaven.

Look at Me, dear child: thousands of Angels surround Me and, reverent, are all in waiting, to hear Me speak of that Divine Fiat whose fount I possess, more than anyone; I know Its admirable secrets, Its infinite joys, Its indescribable happiness and Its incalculable value. To hear my child calling Me, because she wants my lessons on the Divine Will, is the greatest feast for Me - the purest joy; and if you listen to my lessons, I will call Myself fortunate to be your Mother. Oh! how I yearn to have a child who wants to live only of Divine Will. Tell Me, O child, will you make Me content? Will you give Me your heart, your will, all of yourself, into my maternal hands, that I may prepare you, dispose you, fortify you, empty you of everything, so as to be able to fill you completely with the light of the Divine Will, and form in you Its Divine Life? Place your head upon the Heart of your Celestial Mother, and be attentive in listening to Me, so that my sublime lessons may make you decide never to do your will, but always that of God. My child, listen to Me: it is my maternal Heart that loves you very much, and wants to pour Itself upon you. Know that I have you here, inscribed in my Heart, and that I love you as my true child. But I feel a sorrow, because I do not see you as similar to your Mother. Do you know what renders us dissimilar? Ah! It is your will that takes away from you the freshness of grace, the beauty that enamors your Creator, the strength that conquers and bears everything, the love that consumes everything. In sum, it is not that Will which animates your Celestial Mother. You must know that I knew my human will only to keep it sacrificed in homage to my Creator. My life was all of Divine Will; from the first instant of my Conception, I was molded, warmed and placed into Its light, which purified my human seed with Its power, in such a way that I was conceived without original sin. Therefore, if my Conception was spotless and so glorious as to form the honor of the Divine Family, it was only because the Omnipotent Fiat poured Itself upon my seed, and I was conceived pure and holy. So, if the Divine Will had not poured Itself upon my seed more than a tender mother, in order to prevent the effects of original sin, I would have encountered the sad destiny of the other creatures, of being conceived with original sin. Therefore, the primary cause was, entirely, the Divine Will; to It be honor, glory, thanksgiving, for my having been conceived without original sin.

Now, child of my Heart, listen to your Mother: banish your human will; content yourself with dying rather than concede to it one act of life. Your Celestial Mother would have been content with dying thousands and thousands of times, rather than do one single act of my will; don't you want to imitate Me? Ah! If you keep it sacrificed in honor of your Creator, the Divine Will will take the first step in your soul, and you will feel molded with a celestial aura, purified and warmed, in such a way as to feel the seeds of your passions being annihilated; and you will feel placed in the first steps of the Kingdom of the Divine Will. Therefore, be attentive; if you are faithful in listening to Me, I will guide you, I will lead you by the hand along the interminable ways of the Divine Fiat; I will keep you sheltered under my blue mantel, and you will be my honor, my glory, my victory and yours.

The soul:

Immaculate Virgin, take me on your maternal knees, and be my Mother. With your holy hands, take possession of my will; purify it, mold it, warm it by the touch of your maternal fingers. Teach me to live only of Divine Will.

Little Sacrifice:

Today, to honor Me, from the morning, and in all your actions, you will place your will into my hands, saying to Me: "My Mother, You Yourself offer the sacrifice of my will to my Creator."

Ejaculatory Prayer:

My Mother, enclose the Divine Will in my soul, that It may take Its first place, and form in it Its throne and Its dwelling.

Day Two

The Second Step of the Divine Will in the Queen of Heaven.

The First Smile of the Sacrosanct Trinity over Her Immaculate Conception.

The soul:

Here I am again upon your maternal knees, to listen to your lessons. Celestial Mother, this poor child entrusts herself to your power. I am too poor, I know; but I know that You love me as a Mother, and this is enough for me to fling myself into your arms, that You may have compassion for me; and opening the ears of my heart, You will let me hear your most sweet voice, to give me your sublime lessons. You, Holy Mother, will purify my heart by the touch of your maternal fingers, that I may enclose in it the celestial dew of your celestial teachings.

Lesson of the Queen of Heaven:

My child, listen to Me: if you knew how much I love you, you would trust your Mother more, and would let not even a word of mine escape you. You must know that I not only keep you inscribed in my Heart, but inside this Heart I have a maternal fiber that, more than Mother, makes me love my child. Therefore, I want to let you hear the great prodigy that the Supreme Fiat operated in Me, so that you, by imitating Me, may give Me the great honor of being my daughter-queen. How my

Heart, drowned in love, yearns to have around Me the noble cohort of my little queens.

So, listen to Me, my beloved child. As soon as the Divine Fiat poured Itself over my human seed in order to prevent the sad effects of sin, the Divinity smiled, It put Itself in feast in seeing, in my seed, that human seed, pure and holy, just as it came out of Their creative hands in the creation of man. So, the Divine Fiat took the second step in Me, by carrying this human seed of mine, purified and sanctified by It, before the Divinity, that It might pour out in torrents upon my littleness in the act of being conceived. And the Divinity, recognizing in Me Their creative work, beautiful and pure, smiled with satisfaction, and wanting to celebrate Me, the Celestial Father poured upon Me seas of power; the Son, seas of wisdom; the Holy Spirit, seas of love. So I was conceived in the interminable light of the Divine Will; and in the midst of these divine seas, as my littleness could not contain them, I formed gigantic waves, to send them back as homage of love and glory to the Father, to the Son, and to the Holy Spirit.

And the Trinity was all eyes upon Me; and so as not to be surpassed by Me in love, smiling at Me and caressing Me, sent Me more seas, which embellished Me so much, that as soon as my little humanity was formed, I acquired the enrapturing virtue of enrapturing my Creator. And He truly let Himself be enraptured; so much so, that between Me and God it was always feast. We denied nothing to each other - I never denied anything to Them, nor did They. But do you know who animated Me with this enrapturing power? The Divine Will, which reigned in Me as life. The power of the Supreme Being was mine, and therefore We had equal power to enrapture each other.

Now, my child, listen to your Mother: know that I love you very much, and would like to see your soul filled with my same seas. These seas of mine are swollen, and want to pour themselves out; but in order for them to do this, you must empty yourself of your will, so that the Divine Will may take the second step over you, and constituting Itself as origin of life in your soul, It may call the attention of the Celestial Father, of the Son and of the Holy Spirit, to pour Themselves upon you with Their overflowing seas. But in order to do this, They want to find Their own Will in you, because They do not want to entrust Their seas of power, of wisdom and of unspeakable beauty to your human will

Child most dear to Me, listen to your Mother; place your hand upon your heart and tell Me your secrets: how many times have you been unhappy, tortured, embittered, because you have done your will? Know that you have cast a Divine Will out, and have fallen into the maze of evils. The Divine Will wanted to render you pure and holy, happy and beautiful of an enchanting beauty; and you, by doing your own will, have waged war against It, and, in sorrow, you have cast It out of Its dear dwelling, which is your soul.

Listen, child of my Heart, this is a sorrow for your Mother, as I do not see in you the Sun of the Divine Fiat, but the thick darkness of the night of your human will. But, take courage; if you promise Me to place your will into my hands, I, your Celestial Mother, will take you in my arms; I will place you on my knees, and will reorder in you the life of the Divine Will. And so you too, after so many tears, will form my smile, my feast, and the smile and the feast of the Sacrosanct Trinity.

The soul:

Celestial Mother, if You love me so much, I pray You not to allow me to come down from your maternal knees; and as soon as You see that I am about to do my will, watch over my poor soul, and enclosing me in your Heart, let the power of your love burn up my will. In this way, I will change your tears into smiles of delight.

Little Sacrifice:

Today, to honor Me, as many as three times you will come up on my knees, delivering your will to Me, saying to Me: "My Mother, I want this will of mine to be yours, that You may exchange it with the Divine Will."

Ejaculatory Prayer:

Sovereign Queen, with your divine empire, knock down my will, so that the seed of the Divine Will may spring up within me.

Day Three

The Third Step of the Divine Will in the Queen of Heaven. The Smile of all Creation for the Conception of the Celestial Baby.

The soul to the Virgin:

Sovereign Mother, this little child of yours, enraptured by your celestial lessons, feels the extreme need to come each day upon your maternal knees, to listen to You and to place your maternal teachings into my heart. Your love, your sweet accent, your pressing me to your Heart, in your arms, infuse courage in me, and the confidence that my Mother will give me the great grace of making me comprehend the great evil of my will, to make me live of Divine Will.

Lesson of the Queen of Heaven:

My child, listen to Me; it is a heart of mother that speaks to you, and as I see that you want to listen to Me, my Heart rejoices and feels the sure hope that my child will take possession of the Kingdom of the Divine Will, which I possess within my maternal Heart, to give It to my children. Therefore, be attentive in listening to Me, and write all my words within your heart, that you may always meditate on them, and model your life according to my teachings. Listen, my child: as soon as the Divinity smiled and celebrated my Conception, the

21

Supreme Fiat took the third step over my little humanity. Tiny, tiny as I was, It endowed Me with divine reason; and moving all Creation in feast, It made Me be recognized by all created things as their Queen. They recognized in Me the life of the Divine Will, and the whole universe prostrated itself at my feet, though I was tiny and not yet born. And singing my praises, the sun made feast for Me and smiled with its light; the heavens made feast for Me with their stars, which smiled at Me with their meek and sweet twinkling and offered themselves as refulgent crown over my head; the sea made feast for Me with its waves, rising and falling peacefully. In sum, there was not one created thing that did not unite itself to the smile and to the feast of the Sacrosanct Trinity. All accepted my dominion, my rule, my command, and they felt honored because, after so many centuries from the time in which Adam had lost the command and the dominion of king by withdrawing from the Divine Will, they found in Me their Queen; and all Creation proclaimed Me Queen of Heaven and earth.

My dear child, you must know that when the Divine Will reigns in the soul, It does not know how to do small things - but great. It wants to centralize all of Its divine prerogatives in the fortunate creature, and everything that came out of Its Omnipotent Fiat surrounds her and remains obedient to her wishes. What did the Divine Fiat not give to Me? It gave Me everything - Heaven and earth were in my power; I felt dominator of all, and even of my very Creator.

Now, my child, listen to your Mother. Oh! how my Heart grieves in seeing you weak, poor; nor do you have the true dominion of dominating yourself. Fears, doubts, apprehensions, are the things that dominate you – all miserable rags of your human will. But do you know why? Because the life of the Divine Will, intact, is missing in you, which, putting to flight all the evils of the human will, may render you happy and fill you with all the goods It possesses. Ah! if you, with a firm resolution, decide no longer to give life to your human will, you will feel all evils die, and all goods come back to life within you. And then everything will smile at you, and the Divine Will will take the third step, also in you, and all Creation will make feast for the newly arrived in the Kingdom of the Divine Will.

Therefore, my child, tell Me – will you listen to Me? Do you give Me your word that you will never – never again do your will? Know that if you do this, I will never leave you, I will place Myself as guardian of your soul; I will envelope you within my light, so that no one may dare to importune my child. I will give you my rule, that you may rule over all the evils of your will.

The soul:

Celestial Mother, your lessons descend into my heart and fill it with celestial balm. I thank You for lowering Yourself so much toward me, poor little one. But listen, O my Mother - I fear myself; but if You want, You can do anything, and with You, I can do anything. I abandon

23

myself like a little baby in the arms of my Mother, and I am certain that I will satisfy Her maternal yearnings.

Little Sacrifice:

Today, to honor Me, you will look at the heavens, the sun, the earth, and uniting yourself with all, as many as three times, you will recite three Glory Be's in order to thank God for having constituted Me Queen of all.

Ejaculatory Prayer:

Powerful Queen, dominate over my will, to convert it into Divine Will.

Day Four

The Fourth Step of the Divine Will in the Queen of Heaven. The Test.

The soul to the Virgin:

Here I am again, on the maternal knees of my dear Celestial Mother. My heart beats so very strongly. I am restless with love for the desire to hear your beautiful lessons; therefore, give me your hand and take me in your arms. In your arms I spend moments of Paradise – I feel happy. Oh, how I yearn to hear your voice - a new life descends into my heart. Therefore, speak to me, and I promise to put your holy teachings into practice.

Lesson of the Queen of Heaven:

My child, if you knew how much I love to hold you tightly in my arms, leaning on my maternal Heart, to let you hear the celestial secrets of the Divine Fiat.... And if you yearn so much to listen to Me, those are my yearnings that echo in your heart; it is your Mother that wants her child, and wants to entrust Her secrets to her, and narrate to you the story of what the Divine Will operated in Me.

Child of my Heart, pay attention to Me; it is my Heart of Mother that wants to pour Itself out with her child. I want to tell you my secrets which, until now, have not been revealed to anyone, because the hour of God had not yet sounded, in which, wanting to bestow surprising graces upon creatures, which He has not conceded in the whole history of the world, He wants to make known the prodigies of the Divine Fiat - what It can operate in the creature, if she lets herself be dominated by It. And this is why He wants to place Me in the sight of all, as model, since I had the great honor of forming my whole life of Divine Will.

Now, my child, know that as soon as I was conceived and put the Divinity in feast, Heaven and earth made feast for Me, and recognized Me as their Queen. I remained so identified with my Creator, that I felt Myself as the owner in the divine dominions. I did not know what separation from my Creator was; that same Divine Will which reigned in Me, reigned in Them, and rendered Us inseparable. And while everything was smile and feast between Me and Them, I could see that They could not trust Me if They did not receive a proof. My child, the test is the flag that says victory; the test places all the goods that God wants to give us in safekeeping; the test matures and disposes the soul for gains of great conquests. And I too saw the necessity of this test, because I wanted to give proof to my Creator, in exchange for the so many seas of graces He had given Me, with an act of my faithfulness which would cost Me the sacrifice of my whole life. How beautiful it is to be able to say: "You have loved me, I have loved You" - but without the test, it can never be said.

Now, know, my child, that the Divine Fiat made known to Me the creation of man, innocent and holy. For him too everything was happiness; he had command over all Creation, and all the elements were obedient to his wishes. Since the Divine Will was reigning in Adam, by virtue of It, he too was inseparable from his Creator. After the so many goods that God had given him, in order to receive one act of faithfulness in Adam, He commanded him not to touch one fruit only, of the many which were there in the terrestrial Eden. This was the proof that God wanted in order to confirm his innocence, sanctity and happiness, and to give him the right of command over the whole of Creation. But Adam was not faithful in the test, and because he was not faithful, God could not trust him. And so he lost command, innocence and happiness, and it can be said that he turned the work of Creation upside down.

Now know, child of my Heart, that in knowing the grave evils of the human will in Adam and in all his progeny, I, your Celestial Mother, though newly conceived, cried bitterly and with hot tears over fallen man. And the Divine Will, in seeing Me cry, asked Me, as proof, to surrender my human will to It. The Divine Fiat said to Me: "I do not ask of you a fruit, as with Adam; no, no – but I ask you for your will. You will keep it as if you did not have it, under the empire of my Divine Will, which will be your life, and will feel confident to make of you whatever It wants." So, the Supreme Fiat took the fourth step in my soul, asking Me for my will as proof, waiting for my Fiat, and for my acceptance of such a test.

Tomorrow I will wait for you again to come upon my knees, to let you hear the outcome of the test; and since I want you to imitate your Mother, I pray you, as Mother, never to deny anything to your God, be they even sacrifices that would last your whole life. Remaining ever unwavering in the test which God asks of you, your faithfulness, is the call of the divine designs upon you; it is the reflection of His virtues which, like many brushes, make of the soul the masterpiece of the Supreme Being. It can be said that the test offers the material into the divine hands, for Them to accomplish Their crafting in the creature. God does not know what to do with one who is not faithful in the test; not only this, but he upsets the most beautiful works of his Creator.

Therefore, my dear child, be attentive: if you are faithful in the test, you will make your Mother happier. Do not cause Me to be worried, give Me your word, and I will guide you and sustain you in everything as my child.

The soul:

Holy Mother, I know my weakness, but your maternal goodness infuses such confidence in me that I hope for everything from You, and with You I feel secure. Even more, I place into your maternal hands the very tests which God will dispose for me, that You may give me all those graces so that I may not send the divine designs to ruin.

Little Sacrifice:

Today, to honor Me, you will come three times onto my maternal knees, and will bring Me all your pains, of soul and of body. You will bring everything to your Mother, and I will bless them for you, in order to infuse in them the strength, the light, the grace that are needed.

Ejaculatory Prayer:

Celestial Mother, take me into your arms, and write in my heart: "Fiat, Fiat, Fiat."

Day Five

The Fifth Step of the Divine Will in the Queen of Heaven. The Triumph of the Test.

The soul to the Virgin:

Celestial Sovereign, I see that You stretch out your arms toward me, to take me onto your maternal knees; and I run – or rather, I fly, to enjoy the chaste embraces, the celestial smiles of my Celestial Mother. Holy Mother, your appearance today is of a triumpher, and with an air of triumph You want to narrate to me the triumph of your test. Ah! yes, most gladly I will listen to You, and I pray You to give me the grace to be able to triumph in the tests which the Lord will dispose for me.

Lesson of the Queen of Heaven:

Child most dear to Me, oh! how I yearn to confide my secrets to my child; secrets which will give Me much glory, and which will glorify that Divine Fiat which was the primary cause of my Immaculate Conception, of my Sanctity, Sovereignty and Maternity. I owe everything to the Fiat – I know nothing else. All of my sublime prerogatives for which the Holy Church so much honors Me, are nothing other than the effects of that Divine Will which dominated Me, reigned and lived in Me. This is why I yearn so much that That which produced in Me so many privileges and admirable effects as to astonish Heaven and earth, be known.

Now listen to Me, dear child: as soon as the Supreme Being asked Me for my human will, I comprehended the grave evil that the human will can do in the creature, and how it puts everything in danger, even the most beautiful works of her Creator. The creature, with her human will, is all oscillation; she is weak, inconstant, disordered. And this, because in creating man, God had created him united with His Divine Will as though by nature, in such a way that It was to be the strength, the prime motion, the support, the food, the life of the human will. So, by not giving life to the Divine Will in our own, we reject the goods received from God in creation, and the rights received, by nature, in the act in which we were created.

Oh! how well I comprehended the grave offense that is given to God, and the evils that pour upon the creature. I had such horror and fear of doing my will - and rightly did I fear, because Adam too was created innocent by God, and yet, by doing his own will, into how many evils did he not plunge himself and all generations?

Therefore, I, your Mother, taken by terror, and even more, by love toward my Creator, swore never to do my will. And to be more sure and to better attest my sacrifice to the One who had given Me so many seas of graces and privileges, I took this human will of mine and I bound it to the foot of the Divine Throne, in continuous homage of love and sacrifice, promising never to use my will, not even for one instant of my life, but always that of God.

My child, to you, perhaps, my sacrifice of living without my will may not seem great; but I tell you that there is no sacrifice similar to mine – even more, all other sacrifices in the whole history of the world can be called shadows in comparison with mine. To sacrifice oneself for one day – now yes, now no – is easy; but to sacrifice oneself in each instant, in each act, in the very good that one wants to do, for one's entire life, without ever giving life to one's own will, is the sacrifice of sacrifices; it is the greatest attestation that can be offered, and the purest love, filtered through the Divine Will Itself, that can be offered to our Creator. This sacrifice is so great, that God cannot ask anything more of the creature, nor can she find how to sacrifice more for her Creator.

Now, my most dear child, as soon as I gave the gift of my will to my Creator, I felt triumphant in the test asked of Me, and God felt triumphant in my human will. God was waiting for my proof – that is, a soul who would live without will – in order to adjust the balance with mankind, and to assume the attitude of clemency and mercy.

Therefore, I will wait for you again to narrate to you the story of what the Divine Will did after the triumph of the test.

And now, a little word to you, my child: if you knew how I yearn to see you living without your will…. You know that I am your Mother, and a Mother wants to see her child happy; but how can you be happy if you do not decide to live without your will, as your Mother lived?

If you do so, I will give you everything; I will place Myself at your disposal, I will be all for my child, provided that I receive the good, the contentment, the happiness, of having a child who lives all of Divine Will.

The soul:

Triumphant Sovereign, into your hands of Mother do I place my will, so that You Yourself, as Mother, may purify it and embellish it for me, and bind it together with your own to the foot of the Divine Throne, that I may live not with my will, but always – always with that of God.

Little Sacrifice:

Today, to honor Me, in each act you do, you will deliver your will into my maternal hands, and will pray Me to let the Divine Will flow in place of your own.

Ejaculatory Prayer:

Triumphant Queen, steal my will from me, and grant me the Divine Will.

Day Six

The Sixth Step of the Divine Will in the Queen of Heaven. After the Triumph in the Test, the Possession.

The soul to the Virgin:

Queen Mother, I see that You are waiting for me again, and stretching out your hand toward me, You take me on your knees and press me to your Heart, to let me feel the Life of that Divine Fiat which You possess. Oh! how refreshing is Its warmth; how penetrating Its light. O please! Holy Mother, if You love me so much, plunge the little atom of my soul into that Sun of the Divine Will which You conceal, so that I too may be able to say: "My will is ended, it will have life no more; my life will be the Divine Will."

Lesson of the Queen of Heaven:

Dearest child, trust your Mother and pay attention to my lessons; they will serve you to make you abhor your will, and to make you long within yourself for that Holy Fiat, whose Life I so much yearn to form in you.

My child, you must know that the Divinity was assured about Me through the test It wanted - while everyone believes that I did not have any test, and that it was enough for God to make the great portent He made of Me, of conceiving Me without original sin. Oh, how they deceive themselves. On the contrary, He asked of Me a proof which He has asked of no one. And He did this with justice and with highest wisdom, because, since the Eternal Word was to descend into Me, not only was it not decorous that He find in Me the original sin, but it was also not decorous for Him to find in Me a human will operating. It would have been too unseemly for God to descend into a creature in whom reigned the human will. And this is why He wanted from Me, as proof, and for my whole life, my will, in order to secure the Kingdom of the Divine Will within my soul. Once He secured this in Me, God could do with Me whatever He wanted; He could give Me anything, and I can say that He could deny Me nothing.

For now, let us go back to the point we reached. I will reserve the narration of what this Divine Will did in Me during the course of my lessons. Now listen, my child: after the triumph in the test, the Divine Fiat took the sixth step in my soul by having Me take possession of all of the divine properties, as much as it is possible and imaginable for the creature. Everything was mine – Heaven, earth, and even God Himself, whose very Will I possessed. I felt I was the possessor of Divine Sanctity, of Love, of Beauty, Power, Wisdom and Goodness. I felt I was Queen of everything; nor did I feel a stranger in the house of my Celestial Father. I felt vividly His Paternity and the supreme happiness of being His faithful daughter. I can say that I grew up on the paternal knees of God, nor did I know other love or other science but that which my Creator administered to Me. Who can tell you what this Divine Will did in Me?

It elevated Me so high, It embellished Me so much, that the very Angels remain mute, nor do they know where to begin to speak about Me.

Now, my dearest child, you must know that, as soon as the Divine Fiat had Me take possession of everything, I felt Myself the possessor of everything and of everyone. With Its Power, Immensity and All-seeingness, the Divine Will enclosed all creatures in my soul, and I felt a little place in my maternal Heart for each one of them. From the moment I was conceived, I carried you in my Heart, and – oh, how much I loved you, and I love you. I loved you so much, that I acted as your Mother before God; my prayers, my sighs, were for you; and in the delirium of Mother, I said: "Oh! how I wish to see my child possessor of everything, just as I am." Therefore, listen to your Mother: do not want to recognize your human will any more. If you do so, everything will be in common between Me and you; you will have a divine strength in your power; all things will turn into divine sanctity, love and beauty. And in the ardor of my love, just as the Most High sang my praises, "All beautiful, all holy, all pure are You, O Mary!", I will say: "Beautiful, pure and holy is my child, because she possesses the Divine Will."

The soul:

Queen of Heaven, I too hail You: "All beautiful, pure and holy is my Celestial Mother". O please! I pray You, if You have a place for me in your maternal Heart, O please, enclose me in It, so I will be sure that I will not do my will any more, but always that of God; and we, Mother and child, will both be happy.

Little Sacrifice:

Today, to honor Me, you will recite three Glory Be's for three times, in thanksgiving to the Most Holy Trinity for establishing in Me the Kingdom of the Divine Will, giving Me possession of everything. And making the words of the Supreme Being your own, at each Glory Be, you will say to Me: "All beautiful, pure and holy is my Mother."

Ejaculatory Prayer:

Queen of Heaven, make me be possessed by the Divine Will.

Day Seven

**The Queen of Heaven in the Kingdom of
the Divine Will
takes the Scepter of Command, and the Sacrosanct
Trinity constitutes Her Its Secretary.**

The soul to the Divine Secretary:

Queen Mother, here I am, prostrate at your feet. I feel
that, as your child, I cannot be without my Celestial
Mother; and even though today You come to me with
the glory of the scepter of command and with the crown
of Queen, yet You are always my Mother. So, though
trembling, I fling myself into your arms, that You may
heal the wounds which my bad will has made to my
poor soul. Listen, my Sovereign Mother, if You do not
make a prodigy – if You do not take your scepter of
command in order to guide me and hold your empire
over all my acts, so that my will may have no life – alas!
I will not have the beautiful destiny of coming into the
Kingdom of the Divine Will.

Lesson of the Queen of Heaven:

My dear child, come into the arms of your Mother, and
pay attention in listening to Me; and you will hear the
unheard-of prodigies that the Divine Fiat did in your
Celestial Mother.

As I took possession of the Kingdom of the Divine Will,
Its steps within Me ended; more so, since these six steps
symbolized the six days of Creation: each day, by

pronouncing a Fiat, God took as though a step, passing from the creation of one thing to another. On the sixth day, He took the final step, saying: "Fiat - let Us make man in Our image and likeness." And on the seventh day He rested in His works, as though wanting to enjoy everything He had created with such magnificence. And in His rest, looking at His works, He said: "How beautiful are my works - everything is order and harmony." And fixing upon man, in the ardor of His Love, He added: "But you are the most beautiful - you are the crown of all Our works."

Now, my creation surpassed all the prodigies of Creation, and therefore the Divinity wanted to take, with Its Fiat, six steps in Me. As I took possession of the Kingdom of the Divine Will, Its steps in Me ended, and Its full Life, whole and perfect, began within my soul; and - oh! at what divine heights I was placed by the Most High. The heavens could neither reach Me nor contain Me; the light of the sun was small before my light. No created thing could reach Me. I crossed the divine seas as if they were my own; my Celestial Father, the Son and the Holy Spirit, longed for Me to be in Their arms, to enjoy Their little daughter. And, oh! the contentment They felt in feeling that, as I loved Them, prayed Them and adored Their Supreme Height, my love, my prayer and adoration, came out from within my soul, from the center of the Divine Will. They felt, coming out of Me, waves of divine love, chaste fragrances, unusual joys, which started from within the Heaven that Their own Divine Will had formed in my littleness; so much so, that They could not stop repeating: "All beautiful, all pure, all holy, is Our little daughter. Her words are chains that bind Us; Her gazes are darts that wound Us; Her heartbeats are arrows that, darting through Us, make Us go into a delirium of love." They felt the power, the strength of Their Divine Will coming out of Me, which rendered Us inseparable; and They called Me "Our invincible daughter, who will obtain victory even over Our Divine Being."

Now, listen to Me, my child; the Most Holy Trinity, taken by excess of love for Me, told me: "Our beloved daughter, Our Love cannot resist; It feels suffocated if We do not entrust to You Our secrets. Therefore We elect You Our faithful Secretary; to You We want to entrust Our sorrows and Our decrees. At any cost We want to save man - look how he goes toward the precipice. His rebellious will drags him continuously toward evil. Without the life, the strength and the support of Our Divine Will, he has deviated from the path of his Creator, and walks crawling on the earth – weak, ill, and full of all vices. But there are no other ways to save him, nor other ways out, than for the Eternal Word to descend, take his guise, his miseries, his sins upon Himself; become his brother, conquer him by dint of love and unheard-of pains, and give him so much confidence as to be able to bring him back again into Our paternal arms. Oh! how We grieve over the destiny of man. Our sorrow is great, nor could We confide it to anyone, because not having a Divine Will to dominate them, they could never comprehend either Our sorrow, or the grave evils of man fallen into sin. To You, who possess Our Fiat, is given the ability to comprehend it. Therefore, to You, as Our own Secretary, We want to unveil Our secrets, and place the scepter of command into your hands, that You may dominate and rule over everything, and your dominion may conquer God and men, bringing them to Us as Our children, generated anew in your maternal Heart."

Who can tell you, dear child, what my Heart felt at these divine speaking? A vein of intense sorrow opened in Me, and I committed Myself, even at the cost of my life, to conquer God and the creature, and to unite them together.

Now, my child, listen to your Mother: I saw you surprised in hearing Me narrate the story of the possession in the Kingdom of the Divine Will. Now know that this destiny is given also to you: if you decide never to do your will, the Divine Will will form Its Heaven in your soul; you will feel the divine inseparability; the scepter of command over yourself, over your passions, will be given to you. You will no longer be slave to yourself, because only the human will puts the poor creature into slavery, clips the wings of her love toward the One who created her, and takes away from her the strength, the support and the confidence to fling herself into the arms of her Celestial Father – in such a way that she is unable to know either His secrets, or the great love with which He loves her, and therefore she lives like a stranger in the house of her Divine Father. What distance the human will casts between Creator and creature!

Therefore, listen to Me - make Me content. Tell Me you will no longer give life to your will, and I will fill you completely with the Divine Will.

The soul:

Holy Mother, help me; don't You see how weak I am? Your beautiful lessons move me to tears, and I cry over my great misfortune of having fallen many times into the maze of doing my own will, detaching myself from that of my Creator. O please, be my Mother, do not leave me to myself. With your power, unite the Divine Will to mine; enclose me in your maternal Heart, in which I will be sure never to do my will.

Little Sacrifice:

Today, to honor Me, you will remain under my mantle, to learn to live under my gaze; and reciting three Hail Marys to Me, you will pray Me to make everyone know the Divine Will.

Ejaculatory Prayer:

Holy Mother, enclose me in your Heart, that I may learn from You to live of Divine Will.

Day Eight

The Queen of Heaven in the Kingdom of the Divine Will receives the Mandate from Her Creator to place in Safety the Destiny of Mankind.

The soul to the Divine Agent:

Here I am with You, Celestial Mother. I feel I cannot be without my dear Mother; my poor heart is restless, and only when I am on your lap like a tiny little one, clasped to your Heart, to listen to your lessons - then do I feel it at peace. Your sweet accent sweetens all my bitternesses, and sweetly binds my will; and placing it like a footstool under the Divine Will, it makes me feel Its sweet empire, Its life, Its happiness.

Lesson of the Celestial Agent:

Dearest child of mine, know that I love you very much; trust your Mother, and be sure that you will obtain victory over your will. If you are faithful to Me, I will take complete responsibility over you – I will act as your true Mother. Therefore, listen to what I did for you before the Most High.

I did nothing other than bring Myself onto the knees of my Celestial Father. I was little, not yet born; but the Divine Will, whose life I possessed, rendered my visits to my Creator accessible to Me. All doors, all ways, were open for Me, nor was I fearful or afraid of Them. Only the human will causes fear, apprehension, distrust, and puts the poor creature far away from the

One who so much loves her, and who wants to be surrounded by His children. So, if the creature is afraid and fears, and does not know how to be as child and Father with her Creator, it is a sign that the Divine Will does not reign in her. And therefore they are the tortured - the martyred ones of the human will. Therefore, never do your will; do not want to torture and martyr yourself by yourself, for this is the most horrible of martyrdoms, without support and without strength.

Listen to Me: I brought Myself into the arms of the Divinity; more so, since They awaited Me, and made feast on seeing Me. They loved Me so much, that when I would appear, They would pour more seas of love and sanctity into my soul. I do not remember ever having departed from Them without Their adding more surprising gifts for Me.

So, while I was in Their arms, I prayed for mankind; and many times, with tears and sighs, I cried for you, my child, and for all. I cried because of your rebellious will, because of your sad lot of seeing yourself reduced to slavery by it, which rendered you unhappy. To see my child unhappy made Me shed bitter tears, to the point of wetting the hands of my Celestial Father with my crying. And the Divinity, moved by my crying, continued telling Me: "Our beloved daughter, your love binds Us, your tears extinguish the fire of Divine Justice; your prayers draw Us so much toward the creatures, that We do not know how to resist You. Therefore, We give to You the mandate to place in safety the destiny of mankind. You will be Our Agent in their midst. To You do We entrust their souls; You will defend Our rights, prejudiced by their sins; You will be in the middle, between them and Us, to restore the balance on both sides. We feel in You the invincible strength of Our Divine Will which, through You, prays and cries. Who can resist You? Your prayers are commands, your tears rule over Our Divine Being. Therefore, forward in your enterprise."

Now, my dearest child, my little Heart felt consumed with love at the loving ways of the divine speaking; and with all my love I accepted Their mandate, saying to Them: "Highest Majesty, I am here in your arms; dispose of Me in whatever way You want. I will lay down even my life - and if I had as many lives for as many as are the creatures, I would put them at their disposal and Yours, to bring them, all safe, into your paternal arms." And without knowing then that I was to be the Mother of the Divine Word, I felt in Me the double Maternity: Maternity toward God, to defend His just rights; Maternity toward creatures, to bring them to safety. I felt Myself Mother of all. The Divine Will which reigned in Me, and which knows not how to do isolated works, brought God and all creatures from all centuries into Me. In my maternal Heart I felt my God offended, wanting to be satisfied, and I felt the creatures under the empire of Divine Justice. Oh! how many tears I shed. I wanted to make my tears descend into each heart, to let everyone feel my Maternity, all of love. I cried for you and for all, my child. Therefore, listen to Me - have pity on my crying. Take my tears in order to extinguish your passions, and to make your will lose life. O please! accept my mandate – that you do always the Will of your Creator.

The soul:

Celestial Mother, my poor heart cannot endure in hearing how much You love me. Ah! You love me so much, to the point of crying for me. I feel your tears descend into my heart, and like many wounds, they wound me and make me comprehend how much You love me. I want to unite my tears to yours, and pray to You, crying, that You never leave me alone, that You watch over me in everything, and even beat me, if necessary. Be my Mother, and I, your little child, will let You do anything with me, so that your mandate may be the welcome one by me, and You may bring me in your arms to our Celestial Father, as the accomplished act of your divine mandate.

Little Sacrifice:

Today, to honor Me, you will give Me your will, your pains, your tears, your anxieties, your doubts and fears, into my maternal hands, so that, as your Mother, I may keep them in deposit within my maternal Heart, as pledges of my child. And I will give you the precious pledge of the Divine Will.

Ejaculatory Prayer:

Celestial Mother, pour your tears into my soul, that they may heal the wounds that my will did to me.

Day Nine

The Queen of Heaven in the Kingdom of the Divine Will is constituted by God Celestial Peacemaker and Bond of Peace between Creator and Creature.

The soul to her Celestial Queen:

Sovereign Lady and my dearest Mother, I see that You call me as You feel the ardor of the love that burns in your Heart, because You want to narrate to me what You did for your child in the Kingdom of the Divine Will. How beautiful it is to see You direct your steps toward your Creator; and as They hear the treading of your feet, They look at You and feel wounded by the purity of your gazes; and They await You in order to be spectators of your innocent smile, to smile at You, and to amuse Themselves with You. O please! Holy Mother, in your joys, in your chaste smiles with your Creator, do not forget your child who lives in the exile, who is so much in need, and whose will, peeping out, would often want to overwhelm me, to snatch me from the Kingdom of the Divine Will.

Lesson of the Queen of Heaven:

Child of my maternal Heart, do not fear, I will never forget you. On the contrary, if you always do the Divine Will and live in Its Kingdom, we will be inseparable, I will always carry you clasped in my hand, to lead you and be your guide, in order to teach you how to live in the Supreme Fiat. Therefore, banish fear; in It, everything is peace and security. The human will is the disturber of souls, and puts in danger the most beautiful works, the holiest things. Everything is unsafe in it: sanctity, virtues, and even the salvation of the soul are in danger; and the characteristic of one who lives of human will is volubility. Who could ever trust one who lets herself be dominated by the human will? No one – neither God, nor man. She looks like those empty reeds that turn at every blow of wind. Therefore, dearest child of mine, if a blow of wind wants to render you inconstant, plunge yourself into the sea of the Divine Will, and come to hide on the lap of your Mother, that I may defend you from the wind of the human will; and holding you tightly in my arms, I may render you firm and confident along the path of Its Divine Kingdom.

Now, my child, follow Me before the Supreme Majesty, and listen to Me. With my rapid flights, I would reach Their divine arms, and upon arriving, I would feel Their overflowing love which, like mighty waves, covered Me with Their love. Oh! how beautiful it is to be loved by God. In this love one feels happiness, sanctity, infinite joys, and one feels so embellished, that God Himself feels enraptured by the striking beauty He infuses in the creature in loving her.

I wanted to imitate Them, and, though little, I did not want to remain behind Their love. So, from the waves of love They had given Me, I would form my waves, in order to cover my Creator with my love. In doing this, I would smile, because I knew that my love could never cover the immensity of Their love. But in spite of this, I would try, and my innocent smile would arise on my lips. The Supreme Being would smile at my smile, making feast and amusing Himself with my littleness.

Now, in the middle of our loving stratagems, I remembered the painful state of my human family upon earth, for I too was of their offspring - and how I grieved and prayed that the Eternal Word would descend and put a remedy to it. And I would say this with such tenderness as to reach the point of changing smile and feast into crying. The Most High was so moved by my tears, more so, since they were the tears of a little one; and pressing Me to the divine bosom, They dried my tears and said to Me: "Daughter, do not cry, pluck up courage. Into your hands We have placed the destiny of mankind; We gave You the mandate, and now, to console You more, We make of You the Peacemaker between Us and the human family. So, to You it is given to reconcile us. The power of Our Will that reigns in You compels Us to give the kiss of peace to poor humanity, decayed and unsafe." Who can tell you, my child, what my Heart felt at this divine condescension? My love was so great that I felt faint and, in delirium, I was restless, looking for more love as relief for my love.

Now a word to you, my child. If you listen to Me by banishing your will and giving the royal place to the Divine Fiat, you too will be loved with striking love by your Creator; you will be His smile, you will put Him in feast, and will be bond of peace between the world and God.

The soul:

Beautiful Mother, help your child. You Yourself, place me into the sea of the Divine Will, and cover me with the waves of the eternal love, that I may see and hear nothing but Divine Will and love.

Little Sacrifice:

Today, to honor Me, you will ask Me for all of my acts, and will enclose them in your heart, so that you may feel the strength of the Divine Will that reigned in Me. And then you will offer them to the Most High, to thank Him for all the offices He gave Me in order to save the creatures.

Ejaculatory Prayer:

Queen of Peace, make the Divine Will give me Its kiss of peace.

Day Ten

The Queen of Heaven in the Kingdom of the Divine Will, Dawn that rises to put to Flight the Night of the Human Will. Her Glorious Birth.

The soul to the Queen of Heaven:

Here I am, O Holy Mother, near your cradle, to be spectator of your prodigious birth. The heavens are stupefied, the sun is fixed upon You with its light, the earth exults with joy and feels honored to be inhabited by its little newborn Queen; the Angels compete among themselves in surrounding your cradle, to honor You and to be ready for your wishes. So, all honor You and want to celebrate your birth. I too unite myself with all, and prostrate before your cradle, where I see, as though enraptured, your mother Anne and your father Joachim, I want to tell You my first word, I want to entrust to You my first secret. I want to empty my heart into Yours, and say to You: "My Mother, You who are the dawn, herald of the Divine Fiat upon the earth, O please! put to flight the gloomy night of the human will in my soul and in the whole world. Ah! yes, may your birth be our hope which, like a new dawn of grace, may regenerate us in the Kingdom of the Divine Will."

Lesson of the Newborn Queen:

Child of my Heart, my birth was prodigious; no other birth can be said to be similar to mine. I enclosed within Myself the Heaven, the Sun of the Divine Will, and also the earth of my humanity but a blessed and holy earth, which enclosed the most beautiful flowerings. And even though I was just newly born, I enclosed the prodigy of the greatest prodigies: the Divine Will reigning in Me, which enclosed in Me a Heaven more beautiful, a Sun more refulgent than those of Creation, of which I was also Queen, as well as a sea of graces without boundaries, which constantly murmured: "Love, love to my Creator." Therefore, my birth was the true dawn that puts to flight the night of the human will; and as I kept growing, I formed the daybreak and called for the brightest daylight, to make the Sun of the Eternal Word rise over the earth.

My child, come into my cradle to listen to your tiny little Mother. As soon as I was born, I opened my eyes to see this low world, to go in search of all my children in order to enclose them in my Heart, give them my maternal love and, regenerating them to the new life of love and of grace, give them the step to let them enter into the Kingdom of the Divine Fiat, of which I was the possessor. I wanted to act as Queen and as Mother, enclosing everyone in my Heart, to place everyone in safety, and give them the great gift of the Divine Kingdom. In my Heart I had a place for everyone, because for one who possesses the Divine Will there are no constraints, but infinite expanses. Therefore I looked also at you, my child - no one escaped Me. And since on that day everyone celebrated my birth, it was also feast for Me. But upon opening my eyes to the light, I had the sorrow of seeing the creatures in the thick night of the human will.

Oh! in what an abyss of darkness the creature who lets herself be dominated by her will finds herself enwrapped. It is the true night - but a night with no stars; at most, a few fleeting lightnings, which are easily followed by thunders which, in roaring, thicken the darkness even more, and unload the storm over the poor creature – storms of fear, of weaknesses, of dangers, of falling into evil.

My little Heart remained pierced in seeing my children in this horrible storm, in which the night of the human will had overwhelmed them.

Now listen to your little Mother: I am still in the cradle, I am little; look at my tears that I shed for you. Every time you do your will, it is a night that you form for yourself; and if you knew how much this night harms you, you would cry with Me. It makes you lose the light of the day of the Holy Will, it turns you upside down, it paralyzes you to good, it breaks true love in you, and you remain like a poor ill one, who lacks the necessary things to get well Ah! my child, dear child, listen to Me: never do your will; give Me your word that you will make your tiny little Mother content.

The soul:

Holy little Mother, I feel myself trembling in hearing of the ugly night of my will. Therefore I am here, at your cradle, to ask of You the grace that, by your prodigious birth, You make me be reborn in the Divine Will. I will be always near You, Celestial little Baby; I will unite my prayers and my tears to yours, to impetrate, for myself and for all, the Kingdom of the Divine Will upon earth.

Little Sacrifice:

Today, to honor Me, you will come three times to visit Me in my cradle, saying to Me each time: "Celestial little Baby, make me be reborn together with You in the life of the Divine Will."

Ejaculatory Prayer:

My little Mother, make the dawn of the Divine Will rise within my soul.

Day Eleven

The Queen of Heaven in the Kingdom of the Divine Will, in the first Years of Her Life down here, forms a Most Refulgent Daybreak, to make the longed-for Day of Light and of Grace rise in the Hearts.

The soul to the Little Baby Queen:

Here I am again near your cradle, Celestial little Mother. My little heart feels charmed by your beauty and I am unable to detach my gaze from a beauty so rare. How sweet is your gaze; the motion of your little hands calls me to embrace You and to cling to press myself to your Heart, which is drowned with love. Holy little Mother, give me your flames, that they may burn away my human will, and so I can make You content, living of Divine Will together with You.

Lesson of the Queen of Heaven:

My child, if you knew how my maternal little Heart rejoices in seeing you near my cradle to listen to Me…. I feel Myself, with facts, Queen and Mother, because in having you near Me, I am not a sterile Mother or a Queen without a people, but I have my dear child who loves Me very much, and who wants Me to do for her the office of Mother and of Queen. Therefore, you are the bearer of joy to your Mother; more so, since you come onto my lap to be taught by Me how to live in the

Kingdom of the Divine Will. To have a child who wants to live together with Me in this Kingdom so holy is the greatest glory, honor and feast for your Mother. Therefore, pay attention to Me, my dear child, and I will continue to narrate to you the wonders of my birth.

My cradle was surrounded by Angels, who competed among themselves in singing lullabies to Me, as to their sovereign Queen. And since I was endowed with reason and with science, infused in Me by my Creator, I did my first duty to adore, with my intelligence, and also with my babbling little voice of a baby, the Most Holy Adorable Trinity. And the ardor of my love for a Majesty so holy was so great that, feeling Myself languishing, I was delirious for wanting to be in the arms of the Divinity, to receive Their embraces, and to give Them my own. And so the Angels, for whom my desires were commands, picked Me up, and carrying Me on their wings, brought Me into the loving arms of my Celestial Father. Oh! with how much love They awaited Me. I was coming from the exile, and the brief pauses of separation between Me and Them were the cause of new fires of love; they were new gifts that They prepared for Me, to give them to Me; and I would find new devices to ask for pity and mercy for my children who, living in the exile, were under the lash of Divine Justice. And dissolving Myself all in love, I said to Them: "Adorable Trinity, I feel happy - I feel Myself Queen, nor do I know what unhappiness and slavery is. On the contrary, because of your Will reigning in Me, the joys, the happinesses, are so great and so many that, little as I am, I cannot embrace them all. But in so much happiness, there is a vein of intense bitterness in my little Heart: I feel in It my children unhappy, slave to their rebellious will. Have pity, Holy Father – have pity. O please! make my happiness whole - make happy these unhappy children, whom I carry, more than Mother, within my maternal Heart. Let the Divine Word descend upon earth, and everything will be granted. And I will not come down off of your paternal knees if You do not give Me the deed of grace, that I may bring to my children the good news of their Redemption."

The Divinity was moved at my prayers, and filling Me with new gifts, They said to Me: "Return to the exile and continue your prayers. Extend the Kingdom of Our Will in all your acts, for at the appropriate time We will make You content." But They did not tell Me either when or where He would descend.

So I would depart from Heaven only to do the Divine Will. This was the most heroic sacrifice for Me, but I did it gladly, so that the Divine Will alone might have full dominion over Me.

Now listen to Me, my child. How much did your soul cost Me, to the point of embittering the immense sea of my joys and happinesses. Every time you do your will, you render yourself a slave, and you feel your unhappiness; and I, as your Mother, feel in my Heart the unhappiness of my child. Oh! how sorrowful it is to have unhappy children. And how you should take to heart doing the Divine Will, since I reached the point of departing from Heaven so that my will might have no life in Me.

Now, my child, continue to listen to Me: in each one of your acts, may your first duty be to adore your Creator, to know Him and to love Him. This places you in the order of Creation, and you come to recognize the One who created you. This is the holiest duty of each creature: to recognize her origin.

Now you must know that my bringing Myself to Heaven, descending, praying, formed the daybreak around Me, which, spreading in the whole world, surrounded the hearts of my children, so that, from the dawn, the daybreak might rise, to make arise the serene day of the awaiting of the Divine Word upon earth.

The soul:

Celestial little Mother, in seeing You, just newly born, giving me lessons so holy, I feel enraptured and I comprehend how much You love me, to the point of rendering Yourself unhappy because of me. O please! Holy Mother, You who love me so much, let the power, the love, the joys that inundate You, descend into my heart, so that, filled with them, my will may find no room to live in me, and may freely give up the place to the dominion of the Divine Will.

Little Sacrifice:

Today, to honor Me, you will do three acts of adoration to your Creator, reciting three Glory Be's to thank Him for the many times I received the grace to be admitted to Their presence.

Ejaculatory Prayer:

Celestial Mother, make the daybreak of the Divine Will rise within my soul.

Day Twelve

The Queen of Heaven in the Kingdom of the Divine Will leaves the Cradle, takes Her first Steps, and with Her childlike Acts, calls God to descend upon Earth, and calls the Creatures to live in the Divine Will.

The soul to the Celestial Little Queen:

Here I come again to You, my dear little Baby, in the house of Nazareth. I want to be spectator of your tender age; I want to give You my hand as You take your first steps and speak with your holy Mother and with your father Joachim. Little as You are, after you have learned how to walk, You help Saint Anne in the little tasks. My little Mother, how dear You are to me, and all striking. O please! give me your lessons, that I may follow your childhood and learn from You, also in the little human actions, to live in the Kingdom of the Divine Will.

Lesson of the Little Queen of Heaven:

My dear child, my only desire is to keep my child near Me. Without you I feel lonely, and I have no one to whom to confide my secrets. So, it is my maternal cares that seek to have my child near Me, whom I keep in my Heart, in order to give you my lessons, and so make you comprehend how to live in the Kingdom of the Divine Will.

But the human volition does enter into It; it remains crushed and in act of receiving continual deaths before the light, sanctity and power of the Divine Will. But do you think that the human volition remains afflicted because the Divine Will keeps it in the act of dying continually? Ah, no, no - rather, it feels happy that upon its dying will, the Divine Will is born again and rises victorious and triumphant over it, bringing to it joy and happiness without end. It is enough to comprehend, dear child, what it means to let oneself be dominated by It and to experience It, for the creature to abhor her own will so much, that she would rather let herself be torn to pieces than go out of the Divine Will.

Now listen to Me: I departed from Heaven only to do the Will of the Eternal One; and even though I had my Heaven within Me – which was the Divine Will – and I was inseparable from my Creator, yet I enjoyed being in the Celestial Fatherland. More so since, the Divine Will being in Me, I felt my rights of daughter to be with Them, to let Myself be rocked as a tiny little one in Their paternal arms, to participate in all the joys and happiness, riches and sanctity, which They possessed, for as much as I could take of them, and to fill Myself so much, as to be unable to contain any more. And the Supreme Being enjoyed in seeing that, without fear, but rather, with highest love, I filled Myself with Their goods; nor was I surprised that They would let Me take whatever I wanted. I was Their daughter – one was the Will which animated Us; whatever They wanted, I wanted as well. So, I felt that the properties of my Celestial Father were mine. The only difference is that

I was little, and could not embrace or take all Their goods; as many as I would take, so many were left, that I had no capacity to contain them, because I was always a creature; while the Divinity was great – immense, and in one single act It embraced everything.

But, in spite of this, at the moment They would let Me understand that I was to deprive Myself of Their celestial joys and of the chaste embraces which We gave each other, I would depart from Heaven without hesitation, and would return to the midst of my dear parents. They loved Me very much; I was all lovable, striking, cheerful, peaceful, and filled with childlike grace, such as to captivate their affection for Me. They were all attentive over Me - I was their jewel. When they took Me in their arms, they felt unusual things, and a divine life palpitating in Me.

Now, child of my Heart, you must know that as my life down here began, the Divine Will extended Its Kingdom in all my acts. So, my prayers, my words, my steps, the food, the sleep I took, the little tasks with which I helped my mother, were animated by the Divine Will. And since I have always carried you in my Heart, I called you as my child in all my acts. I called your acts to be together with mine, so that also in your acts, even indifferent ones, the Kingdom of the Divine Will might extend. Listen to how much I have loved you: if I prayed, I called your prayer into mine, so that yours and mine might receive the same value and power – the value and the power of a Divine Will. If I spoke, I called your word; if I walked, I called your steps; and if I did the little human actions, indispensable to the human nature – such as taking the water, sweeping, helping my mother by handing the wood to her in order to start the fire, and many other similar things – I called these same acts of yours, that they might receive the value of a Divine Will, and so that, both in mine and in yours, Its Kingdom might extend. And while calling you in each of my acts, I called the Divine Word to descend upon earth.

Oh! how much I have loved you, my child. I wanted your acts within mine in order to render you happy and to let you reign together with Me, and - oh! how many times I called you and your acts, but, to my greatest sorrow, mine remained isolated, and I saw yours as though lost within your human will, forming – horrible to say – the kingdom, not divine, but human: the kingdom of passions, and the kingdom of sin, of unhappinesses and misfortune. Your Mother cried over your misfortune; and for each act of human will that you do, as I know the unhappy kingdom to which they lead you, my tears are still pouring, to make you comprehend the great evil that you do.

Therefore, listen to your Mother: if you do the Divine Will, joys, happinesses, will be given to you by right; everything will be in common with your Creator; weaknesses, miseries, will be banished from you. And then you will be the dearest of my children; I will keep you in my same Kingdom, to let you live always of Divine Will.

The soul:

Holy Mother, who can resist seeing You cry and not listening to your holy lessons? I, with all my heart, promise, swear, never to do my will - never again. And You, Divine Mother – never leave me alone, so that the empire of your presence may crush my will, to let me reign, always – always in the Will of God.

Little Sacrifice:

Today, to honor Me, you will give Me all your acts to keep Me company during my tender age, saying to Me three acts of love, in memory of the three years which I lived with my mother, Saint Anne.

Ejaculatory Prayer.

Powerful Queen, captivate my heart, to enclose it in the Will of God.

Day Thirteen

The Queen of Heaven in the Kingdom of the Divine Will departs for the Temple and gives example of total Triumph in the Sacrifice.

The soul to the Triumphant Queen:

Celestial Mother, today I come to prostrate myself before You, to ask for your invincible strength in all my pains; and You know how my heart is filled with them, to the point of feeling drowned with pains. O please! if You love so much to act as my Mother, take my heart in your hands and pour into it the love, the grace and the strength to triumph in my pains, and to convert them all into Divine Will. Lesson of the Triumphant Queen:

My child, courage, do not fear; your Mother is all for you, and today I was waiting for you so that my heroism and my triumph in the sacrifice may infuse in you strength and courage, that I may see my child triumphant in her pains, with the heroism of bearing them with love and in order to do the Divine Will.

Now, my child, listen to Me: I had just turned three years old when my parents made known to Me that they wanted to consecrate Me to the Lord in the Temple. My heart rejoiced in hearing this – that is, consecrating Myself and spending my years in the house of God. But beneath my joy there was a sorrow - a privation of the dearest persons one can have on earth, which were my dear parents. I was little, I needed their maternal cares; I was depriving Myself of the presence of two great saints. Moreover, I saw that as the day approached on which they were to deprive themselves of Me, who rendered their lives full of joy and of happiness, they felt such bitterness as to feel themselves dying. But, though suffering, they were disposed to make the heroic act of taking Me to the Lord. My parents loved Me in the order of God, and considered Me a great gift, given to them by the Lord; and this gave them the strength to make the painful sacrifice. Therefore, my child, if you want to have invincible strength to suffer the hardest pains, let all your things be in the order of God, and hold them as precious gifts given to you by the Lord.

Now, you must know that I prepared Myself with courage for my departure for the Temple, because, as I delivered my will to the Divine Being and the Supreme Fiat took possession of my whole being, I acquired all virtues as my own nature. I was dominator of Myself; all virtues were in Me like many noble princesses, and according to the circumstances of my life, they promptly showed themselves, to do their office without any resistance. In vain would they have called Me Queen, had I not possessed the virtue of being Queen over Myself. Therefore, I had in my dominion perfect charity, invincible patience, enrapturing sweetness, profound humility, and the whole endowment of the other virtues. The Divine Will rendered my little earth of my humanity fortunate, always flowery, and without the thorns of vices.

Do you see then, dear child, what it means to live of Divine Will? Its light, Its sanctity and power convert all virtues into one's nature; nor does It lower Itself to reign in a soul where there is a rebellious nature - no, no. It is sanctity, and It wants the nature in which It must reign to be ordered and holy. Therefore, by the sacrifice of going to the Temple, it was conquests that I made; and over this sacrifice, the triumph of a Divine Will was formed in Me. And these triumphs brought into Me new seas of grace, of sanctity and of light - to the extent of feeling happy in my pains, in order to be able to conquer new triumphs.

Now, my child, place your hand upon your heart, and tell your Mother: do you feel your nature changed into virtue? Or, do you feel the thorns of impatience, the noxious herbs of agitations, the bad humors of affections which are not holy? Listen – let your Mother do it; place your will into my hands, determined in not wanting it any more, and I will make you be possessed by the Divine Will, which will banish everything from you; and what you have not done in many years, you will do in one day, which will be the beginning of true life, of happiness, and of true sanctity.

The soul:

Holy Mother, help your child; make a visit to my soul, and with your maternal hands, snatch from me everything You find which is not Will of God. Burn away the thorns, the noxious herbs, and You Yourself, call the Divine Will to reign in my soul.

Little Sacrifice:

Today, to honor Me, you will call Me three times to visit your soul, and will give Me all the freedom to do with you whatever I want.

Ejaculatory Prayer:

Sovereign Queen, take my soul in your hands, and transform it completely into Will of God.

Day Fourteen

The Queen of Heaven in the Kingdom of the Divine Will arrives at the Temple, Her Dwelling, and makes Herself Model for Souls consecrated to the Lord.

The soul to the Celestial Queen, Model for Souls:

Celestial Mother, I, your poor child, feel the irresistible need to be with You, to follow your steps, to see your actions in order to copy them, to make of them my model and keep them as guide of my life. I feel so much the need of being guided, because by myself I can do nothing; but with my Mother who loves me so much, I will be able to do everything - and will be able to do also the Divine Will.

Lesson of the Queen of Heaven, Modeller of Souls:

My dear child, it is my ardent desire to let you be spectator of my actions, so that you may be enamored and may imitate your Mother. Therefore, place your hand into mine; I will feel happier to have my child together with Me.

Now, pay attention to Me, and listen. I left the house of Nazareth accompanied by my holy parents. Upon leaving it, I wanted to give one last glance to that little house in which I was born, to thank my Creator for having given Me a place in which to be born, and to leave it in the Divine Will, so that my childhood and so many dear memories – since, being full of reason, I comprehended everything – might all be kept in the Divine Will and deposited in It as pledges of my love toward the One who had created Me.

My child, thanking the Lord and placing our acts into His hands as pledges of our love causes new channels of graces and communications to be opened between God and the soul, and it is the most beautiful homage that one can render to the One who loves us so much. Therefore, learn from Me to thank the Lord for all that He disposes for you, and in anything you are about to do, may your word be: "Thank You, O Lord; I place everything in your hands."

Now, while I left everything in the Divine Fiat, since It reigned in Me and never left Me for one instant of my life, I carried It as though in triumph within my little soul, and – oh! prodigies of the Divine Will - with Its preserving virtue It maintained the order of all my acts, small and great, as though in act within Me, as Its triumph and mine. So, I never lost memory of a single act of mine; and this gave Me so much glory and honor that I felt Queen, because each of my acts done in the Divine Will was more than sun, and I was studded with light, with happiness, with joys. The Divine Will brought Me Its Paradise.

My child, to live of Divine Will should be the desire, the yearning, and almost the passion of all, so great is the beauty that one acquires and the good that one feels. The complete opposite for the human will; it has the virtue of embittering the poor creature; it oppresses her, it forms the night, and she gropes her way, always staggering in good, and many times she loses the memory of the little good she has done.

Now, my child, I departed from my paternal house with courage and detachment, because I looked only at the Divine Will, in which I kept my Heart fixed; and this was enough for Me in everything. But while I was walking to go to the Temple, I looked at all Creation, and – oh! marvel - I felt the heartbeat of the Divine Will in the sun, in the wind, in the stars, in the heavens; even under my steps I felt It palpitating. And the Divine Fiat that reigned in Me commanded all Creation, which concealed It like a veil, to all bow and pay to Me the honor of Queen. And all bowed, giving Me signs of subjection. Even the tiny little flower of the field did not spare itself from giving Me its little homage. I put everything in feast, and when, out of necessity, I would go out of the house, the Creation would place Itself in the act of giving Me signs of honor, and I was forced to command them to remain in their place, and to follow the order of our Creator.

Now, listen to your Mother. Tell Me: do you feel in your heart joy, peace, detachment from everything and from everyone, and the courage that you can do anything in order to fulfill the Divine Will, in such a way as to feel continuous feast within yourself? My child, peace, detachment, courage, form the empty space in the soul in which the Divine Will can take Its place; and being untouchable by any pain, It brings perennial feast into the creature. Therefore, courage my child; tell Me that you want to live of Divine Will, and your Mother will take care of everything. Tomorrow I will wait for you to tell you of the way I conducted Myself in the Temple.

The soul:

My Mother, your lessons enrapture me, and descend deep into my heart. O please! You, who so much love for your child to live of Divine Will, with your empire, empty me of everything; infuse in me the necessary courage to make me give death to my will; and I, trusting in You, will say to You: "I want to live of Divine Will."

Little Sacrifice:

Today, to honor Me, you will give Me all your acts as a pledge of love for Me, saying to Me: "I love You, my Mother"; and I will deposit them in the Divine Will.

Ejaculatory Prayer:

Celestial Mother, empty me of everything, to hide me in the Will of God.

Day Fifteen

The Queen of Heaven in the Kingdom of the Divine Will. Continuing on the same Topic: Her Life in the Temple.

The soul to the Queen of Heaven:

Queen Mother, here I am; your child is at your side to follow your steps as You enter the Temple. Oh! how I wish that my Mother would take my little soul and enclose it in the living Temple of the Will of God, isolating me from everyone, except my Jesus and Her sweet company.

Lesson of the Queen of Heaven:

My dearest child, how sweet is your whispering to my ears – hearing you say that you want to be enclosed by Me in the living Temple of the Divine Will, and that you want no other company but that of your Jesus and mine. Ah! dear child, you make the joys of true Mother arise in my maternal Heart; and if you let Me do it, I am certain that my child will be happy, and my joys will be hers; and to have a happy child is the greatest happiness and glory of a maternal heart.

Now listen to Me, my child: I arrived at the Temple only to live of Divine Will; my holy parents delivered Me to the superiors of the Temple, consecrating Me to the Lord; and while they were doing so, I was dressed up in a festal manner, and hymns and prophecies were sung, which regarded the future Messiah. Oh! how my Heart rejoiced. Afterwards, with courage, I said good-bye to my dear and holy parents; I kissed their right hands, and I thanked them for the care they took of my childhood, and for having consecrated Me to the Lord with so much love and sacrifice. My peaceful presence, without crying and courageous, infused so much courage in them, that they had the strength to leave Me and to depart from Me. The Divine

Will ruled over Me and extended Its Kingdom in all those acts of mine. Oh! power of the Fiat – You alone could give Me the heroism, though I was so little, to have the strength to detach Myself from those who loved Me so much, and whom I saw feeling their hearts break in separating from Me.

Now, my child, listen to Me: I enclosed Myself in the Temple; and the Lord wanted it so, that I might extend the Kingdom of the Divine Will in my acts which I was to do in it, so as to let Me prepare the ground with my human acts, and the Heaven of the Divine Will which was to be formed over this ground, for all souls consecrated to the Lord. I was most attentive to all the duties which were usually done in that holy place. I was peaceful with everyone, nor did I ever cause any bitterness or bother to anyone. I submitted Myself to the most humble tasks; I found no difficulty in anything, either in sweeping or in doing dishes. Any sacrifice was an honor – a triumph for Me. But do you want to know why? I looked at nothing - everything was Will of God for Me. So, the little bell that called Me was the Fiat; I would hear the mysterious sound of the Divine Will which called Me in the sound of the little bell, and my Heart would rejoice and run to go wherever the Fiat was calling Me. My rule was the Divine Will, and I saw my superiors as the ones who imparted the commands of a Will so holy. Therefore, for Me, the little bell, the rule, the superiors, and my actions, even the most humble ones, were joys and feasts which the Divine Fiat prepared for Me; and extending Itself also outside of Me, It called Me to extend Its Will in order to form Its Kingdom in the smallest of my acts. And I acted like the sea, which hides everything it possesses, and lets nothing but water be seen. So I did: I hid everything in the immense sea of the Divine Fiat; I saw nothing but seas of Divine Will, and therefore all things brought Me joys and feasts.

Ah! my child, you and all souls ran within my acts. I could do nothing without my child; it was precisely for my children that I prepared the Kingdom of the Divine Will. Ah! if all the souls consecrated to the Lord in holy places would make everything disappear in the Divine Will, how happy they would be, converting the communities into many celestial families, and populating the earth with many holy souls. But, alas, with the sorrow of Mother, I must say: how many bitternesses, disturbances and discords are not there? – while sanctity is not in the office given to them, but in doing the Divine Will in whatever office that might be entrusted to them, for It is the peacemaker of souls, strength and support in the hardest sacrifices.

The soul:

Oh! Holy Mother, how beautiful are your lessons. How sweetly they descend into my heart. O please! I pray You to extend in me the sea of the Divine Fiat, and to raise it around me like a wall, so that your child may see and know nothing else but Divine Will, in such a way that, journeying always through It, I may know Its secrets, Its joys, Its happiness.

Little Sacrifice:

Today, to honor Me, you will do for Me twelve acts of love, to honor the twelve years which I lived in the Temple, praying Me to admit you to the union with my acts.

Ejaculatory Prayer:

Queen Mother, enclose me in the sacred Temple of the Will of God.

Day Sixteen

The Queen of Heaven in the Kingdom of the Divine Will continues Her Life in the Temple, and forms the New Day to make the Refulgent Sun of the Divine Word rise upon Earth.

The soul to her Celestial Mother:

My most sweet Mother, I feel that You have stolen my heart, and I run to my Mother, who keeps my heart within Hers as pledge of my love, and, in place of my heart, wants to put the Divine Will as pledge of Her love of Mother. Therefore I come into your arms, so that, as your child, You may prepare me, give me your lessons, and do with me whatever You want; and I pray You never to leave your child alone, but to keep me always - always together with You.

Lesson of the Queen of Heaven:

My dearest child, oh, how I long to keep you always together with Me. I would like to be your heartbeat, your breath, the works of your hands, the step of your feet, to make you feel, through Me, how the Divine Will operated in Me. I would like to pour Its life into you. Oh, how sweet, lovable, enchanting and enrapturing It is. Oh! how you would render Me twice as happy, if I had you, my child, under the total empire of that Divine Fiat which formed all my fortune, my happiness, my glory.

Now pay attention to Me, and listen to your Mother who wants to share Her fortune with you. I continued my life in the Temple, but Heaven was not closed for Me; I could go there as many times as I wanted - I had free passage to ascend and descend. In Heaven I had my Divine Family, and I burned and longed to be with Them. The very Divinity awaited Me with great love in order to converse with Me, to be happy and to make Me more happy, more beautiful, more dear in Their eyes. After all, They had not created Me to keep Me far away - no, no. They wanted to enjoy Me as Their daughter; They wanted to hear Me - how my words, animated by the Fiat, had the power to put peace between God and creatures. They loved to be won by Their little daughter, and to hear Me repeat to Them: "Descend – let the Word descend upon earth." I can say that the very Divinity would call Me; and I would run – I would fly into Their midst. Since I had never done my human will, my presence requited Them of the love and the glory of the great work of all Creation, and therefore They entrusted to Me the secret of the history of mankind. And I prayed and prayed again for peace to come between God and man.

Now, my child, you must know that the human will alone closed Heaven, and therefore it was not given to man to penetrate into those celestial regions, or to have a familiar relationship with his Creator. On the contrary, the human will had cast him away from the One who had created him. As soon as man withdrew from the Divine Will, he became fearful, timid; he lost the dominion of himself and of the whole Creation. All the elements, because they were dominated by the Fiat, had remained superior to him and could do harm to him. Man was afraid of everything; and do you think it is trivial, my child, that the one who had been created as king, dominator of everything, reached the point of being afraid of the One who had created him? It is strange, my child, and I would say almost against nature, that a child would be afraid of his father; while it is according to nature that, as one generates, love and trust between father and child are also generated. This can be called the primary inheritance that is due to the child, and the primary right that is due to the father. So, by doing his will, Adam lost the inheritance of his Father; he lost his Kingdom, and rendered himself the laughing stock of all created things.

My child, listen to your Mother, and ponder well the great evil of the human will. It removes the eyes of the soul and makes her become blind, in such a way that everything is darkness and fear for the poor creature. Therefore, place your hand upon your heart and swear to your Mother that you would rather die than do your will. I, by never doing my will, had no fear of my Creator. And how could I be afraid if He loved Me so much? And the Kingdom extended so much within Me, that with my acts I kept forming the full day to make the new Sun of the Eternal Word rise upon earth. And as I saw that the day was being formed, I increased my supplications to obtain the longed-for day of peace between Heaven and earth.

Tomorrow I will wait for you to narrate to you another surprise of my life down here.

The soul:

My Sovereign Mother, how sweet are your lessons. Oh, how they make me comprehend the great evil of my human will. Oh! how many times I too felt within me fear, timidity, and as though far away from my Creator. Ah! it was my human will that reigned in me - not the Divine; and this is why I felt its sad effects.

Therefore, if You love me as your child, take my heart in your hands, and put out of me the fear, the timidity, which prevent my flight toward my Creator, and, in their place, put in me that Fiat which You so much love, and which You want to reign in my soul.

Little Sacrifice:

Today, to honor Me, you will place into my hands every bother, fear, mistrust that you may feel, that I may convert them into Will of God; saying to me, three times: "My Mother, make the Divine Will reign in my soul."

Ejaculatory Prayer:

My Mother, my trust, form the day of the Divine Will in my soul.

Day Seventeen

The Queen of Heaven in the Kingdom of the Divine Will leaves the Temple. Marriage with Saint Joseph.

Divine Mirror to which She calls, to reflect themselves, all those who are called by God to the Marital State.

The soul to her Celestial Mother:

Holy Mother, today more than ever I feel the need to remain clasped in the arms of my Mother, so that that Divine Will which reigns in You may form the sweet enchantment to my will, that It may keep it subdued, and it may not dare to do anything which is not Will of God. Your lessons of yesterday made me comprehend the life imprisonment into which the human will casts the poor creature, and I so much fear that my will may make little escapes from me, and take its place in me again. Therefore I entrust myself to You, my Mother, that You may watch over me so much, that I may be sure to live always of Divine Will.

Lesson of the Queen of Heaven:

Cheer up, my child – have courage and trust in your Mother, and an iron resolution never to give life to your will. Oh! how I would love to hear from your lips: "My Mother, my will is ended, and the Divine Fiat has total empire in me." These are the weapons that make it die continuously, and conquer the Heart of your Mother to use all the loving arts of Mother, so that Her child may live in the Kingdom of Her Mother. For you it will be sweet death, which will give you true life; and for Me it will be the most beautiful victory I will achieve in the Kingdom of the Divine Will. Therefore, have courage and trust in Me. Distrust is of the cowardly, and of those who are not really committed to obtaining victory, and therefore they are always without weapons; and without weapons one cannot win, and is always inconstant and vacillating in doing good.

Now, my child, listen to Me: I continued my life in the Temple and my little escapes up there to my Celestial Fatherland. I had my rights of daughter to make my little visits to my Divine Family which, more than Father, belonged to Me. But what was not my surprise when in one of these visits of mine They made known to Me that it was Their Will for Me to leave the Temple; first, to unite Myself in bond of marriage, according to the custom of those times, to a holy man called Joseph; and to withdraw together with him to live in the house of Nazareth. My child, in this step of my life, in appearance it seemed that God wanted to put Me in a trial. I had never loved anyone in the world, and since the Divine Will extended through my whole being, my human will never had one act of life; therefore, the seed of human love was missing in Me. How could I love a man in the human order, as great a saint as he might be? It is true that I loved everyone, and that my love toward all was so great, that my love of Mother had inscribed them in my maternal Heart, one by one, with indelible characters of fire. But this was all in the order of divine love; and human love, compared to the divine, can be called shadows, shadings - atoms of love. Yet, my child, that which in appearance seemed to be a trial and as though strange for the sanctity of my life, God used in an admirable way in order to fulfill His designs, and to grant Me the grace which I so much longed for – that is, the descent of the Word upon earth. God gave Me the safeguard, the defense, the help, so that no one could talk about Me – about my honesty. Saint Joseph was to be the cooperator, the tutor, who was to take care of that bit of the human which We needed; as well as the shadow of the Celestial Paternity, in which our little Celestial Family on earth was to be formed.

So, in spite of my surprise, immediately I said: "Fiat", knowing that the Divine Will would not harm Me, or prejudice my sanctity. Oh! had I wanted to put in one act of my human will, even in the aspect of wanting to know no man, I would have sent to ruin the plans of the coming of the Word upon earth. Therefore, it is not the diversity of states that prejudices sanctity, but the lack of Divine Will, and of the fulfillment of one's duties to which God calls the creature. All states are holy, marriage too, as long as the Divine Will is present in them, as well as the exact sacrifice of one's duties. But the great part are indolent and lazy, and not only do they not make themselves saints, but they make of their state, some a purgatory, and some a hell.

So, as I learned that I was to leave the Temple, I did not say a word to anyone, waiting for God Himself to move the external circumstances to make Me fulfill His adorable Will, as indeed it happened. The superiors of the Temple called Me and said to Me that it was their will, and also the custom of those times, that I prepare Myself for marriage. I accepted. Miraculously, among many, the choice fell upon Saint Joseph; and so the marriage was formed and I left the Temple.

Therefore, I pray you, child of my Heart, that in all circumstances you take to heart the Divine Will alone, if you want the divine designs to be accomplished over you.

The soul:

Celestial Queen, your child entrusts herself to You. With my trust, I want to wound your Heart; and may this wound always say in your maternal Heart: "Fiat! Fiat! Fiat!" – so your little child always asks from You.

Little Sacrifice:

Today, to honor Me, you will come onto my knees and will recite fifteen Glory Be's to thank the Lord for all the graces He granted Me up to the fifteenth year of my life, especially for having given Me the company of a man so holy, as was Saint Joseph.

Ejaculatory Prayer:

Powerful Queen, give me the weapons to wage battle, to make me conquer the Will of God.

Day Eighteen

The Queen of Heaven in the Kingdom of the Divine Will in the House of Nazareth. Heaven and Earth are about to exchange the Kiss of Peace. The Divine Hour is Near.

The soul to her Queen Mother:

My Sovereign Mother, I am back again to follow your steps. Your love binds me, and like powerful magnet, it keeps me fixed and all intent on listening to the beautiful lessons of my Mother. But this is not enough for me; if You love me as your child, enclose me in the Kingdom of the Divine Will in which You lived and live, and close the doors in such a way that, even if I wanted, I would no longer be able to go out. So, as Mother and child, we will live common life and will both be happy.

Lesson of the Queen of Heaven:

My dearest child, if you knew how I long to keep you enclosed in the Kingdom of the Divine Will.... Each lesson of mine that I give you is fences that it forms to prevent your stepping out; and it is a fortress to wall up your will, that it may comprehend and love being under the sweet empire of the Supreme Fiat. Therefore, be attentive in listening to Me, because this is nothing other than the work that your Mother does in order to entice and captivate your will, and to make the Divine Will conquer you.

Now, my dear child, listen to Me: I departed from the Temple with the same courage with which I entered It, and only to do the Divine Will. I went to Nazareth and I no longer found my dear and holy parents. I went accompanied only by Saint Joseph, and in him I saw my good angel whom God had given Me for my custody, though I had cohorts of Angels that accompanied Me on the journey. All created things made bows of honor for Me; and I, thanking them, gave each created thing my kiss and my greeting as Queen. And so we arrived at Nazareth.

Now, you must know that Saint Joseph and I looked at each other with modesty, and we felt our hearts swollen, because each one wanted to let the other know that we were bound to God with a vow of perennial virginity. Finally, silence was broken, and we both manifested our vow. Oh! how happy we felt; and thanking the Lord, we protested to live together as brother and sister. I was most attentive in serving him; we looked at each other with veneration, and the dawn of peace reigned in our midst. Oh! if all would reflect themselves in Me by imitating Me.... I adapted Myself very much to the ordinary life; I let nothing appear outside of the great seas of grace that I possessed.

Now, listen to Me, my child: in the house of Nazareth I felt ignited more than ever, and I prayed that the Divine Word would descend upon earth. The Divine Will, which reigned in Me, did nothing but invest all my acts with light, with beauty, with sanctity, with power. I felt It was forming the Kingdom of light within Me – but a light that constantly arises; the Kingdom of beauty, sanctity and power that always grows. So, all the divine qualities, which the Divine Fiat extended within Me with Its reigning, brought Me fecundity. The light that invaded Me was so great, that my very humanity would remain so embellished and invested by this Sun of the Divine Will, that it would do nothing but produce celestial flowers. I felt Heaven lowering Itself down to Me, and the earth of my humanity rising; and Heaven and earth embraced, reconciled, to exchange the kiss of peace and of love. The earth disposed itself to produce the seed in order to form the Just One, the Holy One; and Heaven opened to let the Word descend into this seed.

I would do nothing but descend and ascend to my Celestial Fatherland, and throw Myself into the paternal arms of my Celestial Father, saying to Him with the heart: "Holy Father, I cannot endure any longer – I feel enflamed; and while I burn, I feel a powerful strength within Me that wants to conquer You. With the chains of my love I want to bind You in order to disarm You, that You may delay no more; but upon the wings of my love I want to carry the Divine Word from Heaven to earth." And I prayed and cried that He would listen to Me. And the Divinity, conquered by my tears and prayers, assured Me by saying to Me: "Daughter, who can resist You? You have won; the divine hour is near. Return to the earth and continue your acts in the power of my Volition, and by these, all will be shaken, and Heaven and earth will exchange the kiss of peace." But in spite of this, I did not yet know that I was to be the Mother of the Eternal Word.

Now, dear child, listen to Me, and comprehend well what it means to live of Divine Will. By living of It, I formed Heaven and Its Divine Kingdom in my soul. Had I not formed this Kingdom within Me, the Word could never have descended from Heaven to earth. If He descended, it was because He descended into His own Kingdom, which the Divine Will had formed in Me. He found in Me His Heaven, His divine joys; nor would the Word ever have descended into a foreign kingdom – ah, no, no. First He wanted to form His Kingdom in Me, and then descend as victorious into His Kingdom. Not only this, but by living always of Divine Will, I acquired by grace that which in God is by nature: the divine fecundity, in order to form, without the work of a man, the seed to let the Humanity of the Eternal Word germinate from Me. What can the Divine Will operating in a creature not do? Everything, and all possible and imaginable goods. Therefore, may you take to heart that everything be Divine Will in you, if you want to imitate your Mother, and make Me content and happy.

The soul:

Holy Mother, if You want, You can. Just as You had the power to conquer God, to the point of making Him descend from Heaven to earth, You will not lack the power to conquer my will, that it may no longer have life. In You I hope, from You I will obtain everything.

Little Sacrifice:

Today, to honor Me, you will make Me a little visit in the house of Nazareth, and, as homage to Me, you will give Me all your acts, that I may unite them to mine in order to convert them into Divine Will.

Ejaculatory Prayer:

Celestial Empress, bring the kiss of the Will of God to my soul.

Day Nineteen

The Queen of Heaven in the Kingdom of the Divine Will.

The Doors of Heaven open, the Sun of the Eternal Word places Himself on the lookout. He sends His Angel to tell the Virgin that the Hour of God has come.

The soul to her Celestial Mother:

Holy Mother, here I am again on the knees of my Mother. I am your child, who wants to be fed the food of your most sweet word, which brings me the balm to heal the wounds of my miserable human will. My Mother, speak to me; let your powerful words descend into my heart and form a new creation, in order to form the seed of the Divine Will in my soul.

Lesson of the Sovereign Queen:

Dearest child, this is precisely the purpose for which I love so much to let you hear the celestial secrets of the Divine Fiat, the portents It can operate where It reigns completely, and the great harm of one who lets himself be dominated by the human will: that you may love the Divine Will, to let It form Its throne within you, and abhor the human will, to make of it the footstool of the Divine Will, keeping it sacrificed at Its divine feet.

Now, my child, listen to Me: I continued my life in Nazareth; the Divine Fiat continued to expand Its Kingdom within Me. It used my littlest acts, even the most indifferent ones – such as keeping the little house in order, starting the fire, sweeping, and all the tasks that are usually done in the families – to let Me feel Its life palpitating in the fire, in the water, in the food, in the air I breathed – in everything. And investing them, It formed over my little acts seas of light, of grace, of sanctity; because wherever It reigns, the Divine Will has the power to form, from little trifles, new heavens of enchanting beauty. In fact, being immense, It does not know how to do small things, but with Its power It gives value to trifles, and makes of them the greatest things, such as to astonish Heaven and earth. Everything is holy, everything is sacred, for one who lives of Divine Will.

Now, child of my Heart, pay attention to Me and listen: several days before the descent of the Eternal Word upon earth, I could see Heaven opened and the Sun of the Divine Word at Its doors, as though to look out for the one upon whom He was to take His flight, to render Himself Celestial Prisoner of a creature. Oh! how beautiful it was to see Him at the doors of Heaven, as though on the lookout, and to spy the fortunate creature who was to host her Creator! The Sacrosanct Trinity no longer looked at the earth as alien to Them, because there was little Mary who, by possessing the Divine Will, had formed the Divine Kingdom in which He could descend safely, as in His own dwelling, in which He would find Heaven and the many suns of the many acts of Divine Will done in my soul. The Divinity overflowed with love, and removing the mantle of justice which, for so many centuries, They had kept with creatures, They covered Themselves with the mantle of infinite mercy, and decreed among Themselves the descent of the Word, and were in the act of sounding the hour of the fulfillment. At this sound, Heaven and earth were astounded, and all stood at attention, to be spectators of such a great excess of love, and a prodigy so unheard-of.

Your Mother felt ignited with love, and echoing the love of my Creator, I wanted to form one single sea of love, so that the Word might descend upon earth within it. My prayers were incessant, and while I was praying in my little room, an Angel came, sent from Heaven as messenger of the great King. He came before Me, and bowing, he hailed Me: "Hail, O Mary, our Queen; the Divine Fiat has filled You with grace. He has already pronounced His Fiat - that He wants to descend; He is already behind my shoulders, but He wants your Fiat to form the fulfillment of His Fiat."

At such a great announcement, so much desired by Me – although I had never thought I would be the chosen one – I was stupefied and hesitated one instant. But the Angel of the Lord told Me: "Do not fear, our Queen, for You have found grace before God. You have conquered your Creator; therefore, to complete the victory – pronounce your Fiat."

I pronounced my Fiat, and – oh! marvel - the two Fiat fused together and the Divine Word descended into Me. My Fiat, which was endowed with same value as the Divine Fiat, from the seed of my humanity, formed the tiny little Humanity which was to enclose the Word; and the great prodigy of the Incarnation was accomplished.

Oh! power of the Supreme Fiat - You raised Me so high as to render Me powerful, to the point of being able to create within Me that Humanity which was to enclose the Eternal Word, whom Heaven and earth could not contain. The heavens were shaken, and all Creation assumed the attitude of feast; and exulting with joy, they peeked over the little house of Nazareth, to give homages and obsequies to the Creator made Man; and in their mute language, they said: "Oh! prodigy of prodigies, which only a God could do. Immensity has made itself little, power has rendered itself powerless, His unreachable height has lowered itself deep into the abyss of the womb of a Virgin, and at the same time, He is little and immense, powerful and powerless, strong and weak."

My dear child, you cannot comprehend what your Mother experienced in the act of the Incarnation of the Word. All pressed upon Me and awaited my Fiat, I could say, omnipotent.

Now, dear child, listen to Me: how much you should take to heart doing the Divine Will and living of It. My power still exists - let Me pronounce my Fiat over your soul. But in order to do this, I want your own. A true good cannot be done with one alone; the greatest works are always done between two. God Himself did not want to do it on His own, but wanted Me together with Him to form the great prodigy of the Incarnation; and in my Fiat and in His, the life of the Man-God was formed, the destiny of mankind was restored, Heaven was no longer closed; all goods were enclosed between the two Fiat. Therefore, let us pronounce them together: "Fiat, Fiat", and my maternal love will enclose in you the life of the Divine Will. Enough for now; tomorrow I will wait for you again, to narrate to my child the continuation of the Incarnation.

The soul:

Beautiful Mother, I feel stupefied in hearing your beautiful lessons. O please! I pray You to pronounce your Fiat over me; and I will pronounce my own, so that that Fiat, for which You so much yearn to reign as life in me, may be conceived in me.

Little Sacrifice:

Today, to honor Me, You will come to give the first kiss to Jesus, and will say to Him, as many as nine times, that you want to do His Will. And I will repeat the prodigy of making Jesus be conceived in your soul.

Ejaculatory Prayer:

Powerful Queen, pronounce your Fiat, and create in me the Will of God.

Day Twenty[1]

**The Queen of Heaven in the Kingdom of the Divine
Will. The Virgin, Heaven studded with Stars. In
this Heaven, the Sun of the Divine Fiat blazes with
Its Most Refulgent Rays and fills Heaven and earth.
Jesus in the Womb of His Mother.**

The soul to her Mother Queen:

Here I am again with You, my Celestial Mother. I come
to rejoice with You, and bowing at your holy feet, I hail
You, Full of Grace and Mother of Jesus. Oh! I will no
longer find my Mother alone, but I will find my little
Prisoner Jesus together with You. So, we will be three,
no longer two: together, Mother, Jesus and I. What
fortune for me, that if I want to find my little King Jesus,
it is enough to find His Mother and mine. O please! O
Holy Mother, at the height of Mother of a God at which
You are, have pity on your miserable and little child,
and say for me the first word to little Prisoner Jesus –
that He give me the great grace to live of His Divine Will.

Lesson of the Queen of Heaven, Mother of Jesus:

My dear child, today I await you more than ever. My
maternal Heart is swollen; I feel the need to pour out
my ardent love with my child: I want to say to you that
I am the Mother of Jesus. My joys are infinite; seas of
happiness inundate Me. I can say: I am the Mother of
Jesus; His creature, His handmaid, is Mother of Jesus -

95

and I owe this only to the Fiat. It rendered Me full of grace, It prepared the worthy dwelling for my Creator. Therefore, always glory, honor and thanksgiving be to the Supreme Fiat.

Now listen to Me, child of my Heart: as soon as the little Humanity of Jesus was formed in my womb by the power of the Divine Fiat, the Sun of the Eternal Word incarnated Himself in It. I had my Heaven, formed by the Fiat, all studded with most refulgent stars which glittered with joys, beatitudes, harmonies of divine beauty; and the Sun of the Eternal Word, blazing with inaccessible light, came to take His place within this Heaven, hidden in His little Humanity. And since His little Humanity could not contain Him, the center of this Sun remained in It, but Its light overflowed outside, and investing Heaven and earth, It reached every heart. And with Its pounding of light, It knocked at each creature, and with voices of penetrating light, It said to them: "My children, open to Me; give Me a place in your hearts. I have descended from Heaven to earth in order to form my life in each one of you. My Mother is the center in which I reside, and all my children will be the circumference, in which I want to form so many of my lives for as many as are my children." And the light knocked and knocked again, without ever ceasing; and the little Humanity of Jesus moaned, cried, agonized, and within that light which reached into the hearts, He made flow His tears, His moans and His pangs of love and of sorrow.

Now, you must know that a new life began for your Mother. I was aware of everything that my Son was doing. I saw Him devoured by seas of flames of love; each one of His heartbeats, breaths and pains, were seas of love that He unleashed, enveloping all creatures to make them His own by force of love and of sorrow. In fact, you must know that as His little Humanity was conceived, He conceived all the pains He was to suffer, up to the last day of His life. He enclosed all souls within Himself, because, as God, no one could escape Him. His immensity enclosed all creatures, His all-seeingness made them all present to Him. Therefore, my Jesus, my Son, felt the weight and the burden of all the sins of each creature. And I, your Mother, followed Him in everything, and felt within my maternal Heart the new generation of the pains of my Jesus, and the new generation of all the souls whom, as Mother, together with Jesus I was to generate to grace, to light, to the new life which my dear Son came to bring upon earth.

My child, you must know that from the moment I was conceived, I loved you as Mother, I felt you in my Heart, I burned with love for you, but I did not understand why. The Divine Fiat made me do facts, but would keep the secret hidden from Me. But as He incarnated Himself, He revealed the secret to Me, and I comprehended the fecundity of my Maternity – that I was to be not only Mother of Jesus, but Mother of all; and this Maternity was to be formed on the stake of sorrow and of love. My child, how much I have loved you, and I love you.

Now listen to Me, dear child – what extent one can reach, when the Divine Will takes operating life in the creature, and the human will lets It work without impeding Its step. This Fiat, which by nature possesses the generative virtue, generates all goods in the creature; It renders her fecund, giving her maternity over all, over all goods, and over the One who created her. Maternity says and means true love, heroic love, love that is content with dying to give life to the one it has generated. If this is not there, the word maternity is sterile, is empty, and is reduced to words, but does not exist with facts. Therefore, if you, my child, want the generation of all goods, let the Fiat take operating life in you, which will give you the maternity, and you will love everyone with love of mother. And I, your Mother, will teach you how to fecundate in you this maternity, all holy and divine.

The soul:

Holy Mother, I abandon myself in your arms. Oh! how I would like to wet your maternal hands with my tears, to move You to compassion for the state of my poor soul. O please! if You love me as Mother, enclose me in your Heart, let your love burn away my miseries, my weaknesses, and let the power of the Divine Fiat, which You possess as Queen, form Its operating life in me, in such a way that I may be able to say: "My Mother is all for me, and I am all for Her."

Little Sacrifice:

Today, to honor Me, you will thank the Lord as many as three times in the name of all, for He incarnated Himself and made Himself Prisoner in my womb, giving Me the great honor of choosing Me as His Mother.

Ejaculatory Prayer:

Mother of Jesus, be my Mother and guide me on the path of the Will of God.

Day Twenty-one

The Queen of Heaven in the Kingdom of the Divine Will. Rising Sun. Full Midday. The Eternal Word in our Midst.

The soul to her Queen Mother:

Most sweet Mother, my poor heart feels the extreme need to come onto your maternal knees to confide to You my little secrets and to entrust them to your maternal Heart. Listen, oh! my Mother, in looking at the great prodigies that the Divine Fiat operated in You, I feel it is not given to me to imitate You because I am little, weak; and then, the tremendous struggles of my existence, which crush me and leave me but a breath of life.

My Mother, oh, how I would want to pour my heart into Yours, to let You feel the pains that embitter me and the fear that tortures me - that I may fail to do the Divine Will. Have pity, O Celestial Mother, have pity. Hide me in your Heart and I will lose the memory of my evils, to remember only to live of Divine Will.

Lesson of the Queen of Heaven, Mother of Jesus:

Dearest child, do not fear, trust your Mother; pour everything into my Heart, and I will take everything into account. I will be your Mother, I will change your pains into light, and will use them to expand the boundaries of the Kingdom of the Divine Will in your soul.

Therefore, put everything aside for now, and listen to Me; I want to tell you what little King Jesus operated in my maternal womb, and how your Mother did not lose even one breath of little Jesus.

My child, the little Humanity of Jesus kept growing, united hypostatically with the Divinity. My maternal womb was so very narrow, dark - there was not a glimmer of light. And I could see Him in my maternal womb, immobile, enveloped in a deep night. But do you know what formed this darkness, so intense, for the Infant Jesus? The human will, in which man had voluntarily enveloped himself; and for as many sins as he committed, so many abysses of darkness he formed around and within himself, in such a way that it rendered him immobile to doing good. And my dear Jesus, in order to put to flight the darkness of this night so deep, in which man had rendered himself the prisoner of his own tenebrous will, to the point of losing the motion of doing good, chose the sweet prison of His Mother and, voluntarily, exposed Himself to the immobility of nine months.

My child, if you knew how martyred was my maternal Heart in seeing little Jesus in my little womb, immobile, crying, sighing.... His ardent heartbeat palpitated so very strongly; fidgeting with love, He made His heartbeat heard in every heart, to ask them - for pity's sake – for their souls, so as to enclose them in the light of His Divinity, because for love of them He had voluntarily exchanged light for darkness so that all might obtain true light in order to reach safety. My dearest child, who can tell you what my little Jesus suffered in my womb? Unheard-of and indescribable pains. He was endowed with full reason – He was God and Man; and His love was so great that He put as though aside the infinite seas of joys, of happiness, of light, and plunged His tiny Humanity into the seas of darkness, of bitternesses, of unhappiness, of miseries, which creatures had prepared for Him. And little Jesus took them all upon His shoulders, as if they were His own. My child, true love never says 'enough'. It does not look at the pains, and by dint of pains it searches for the loved one; and when it lays down its life to give life back to the beloved - then is it content.

My child, listen to your Mother; see what great evil it is to do your will: not only do you prepare the night for your Jesus and for yourself, but you form seas of bitternesses, of unhappiness and of miseries, in which you remain so engulfed as to be unable to escape. Therefore, be attentive; make Me happy by saying to Me: "I want to do always the Divine Will."

Now listen, my child: little Jesus, in spasms of love, is in the act of taking the step to come out to the light of the day. His yearnings, His ardent sighs and desires for He wants to embrace the creature, to make Himself seen, and to look at her in order to enrapture her to Himself, give Him no more respite. And just as one day He put Himself on the lookout at the doors of Heaven in order to enclose Himself in my womb, so is He now in the act of putting Himself on the lookout at the doors of my womb, which is more than Heaven. And the Sun of the Eternal Word rises in the world and forms in it Its full midday. So, there will be night no longer for the poor creatures, nor dawn, nor daybreak – but always sunshine, more than at the fullness of midday. Your Mother felt She could no longer contain Him within Herself. Seas of light and of love inundated Me; and just as I conceived Him within a sea of light, so within a sea of light He came out of my maternal womb. Dear child, for one who lives of Divine Will everything is light, and everything converts into light.

Enraptured in this light, I awaited to embrace my little Jesus in my arms, and as He came out of my womb, I heard His first loving wailings. The Angel of the Lord placed Him in my arms and I pressed Him so very tightly to my Heart and gave Him my first kiss, and little Jesus gave Me His. Enough for now; tomorrow I will wait for you again, to continue the narration of the birth of Jesus.

The soul:

Holy Mother, oh! how fortunate You are - You are the true blessed one among all women. O please! for the sake of those joys which You experienced when You pressed Jesus to your breast and gave Him your first kiss, I pray You to let me hold little Jesus in my arms for a few instants, that I may give Him contentment by saying to Him that I swear to love Him always – always, and that I want to know nothing but His Divine Will.

Little Sacrifice: Today, to honor Me, you will come to kiss the little feet of Baby Jesus, and you will place your will into His little hands to let Him play and smile.

Ejaculatory Prayer: My Mother, enclose little Jesus in my heart, that He may transform it completely into Will of God.

Day Twenty-two

The Queen of Heaven in the Kingdom of the Divine Will. Little King Jesus is Born. The Angels point to Him and call the Shepherds to adore Him. Heaven and Earth exult, and the Sun of the Eternal Word, following Its Course, dispels the Night of Sin and gives rise to the Full Day of Grace. The Home of Bethlehem.

The soul to her Celestial Mother:

Today, Holy Mother, I feel an ardor of love, and I feel that I cannot be without coming onto your maternal knees to find the Celestial little Baby in your arms. His beauty enraptures me, His gazes wound me, His lips, in the act of moaning and bursting into tears, capture my heart to love Him. My dearest Mother, I know that You love me, and therefore I ask You to give me a little place in your arms, so that I may give Him my first kiss, pour my heart into little King Jesus, and entrust to Him my interesting secrets, which so much oppress me. And in order to make Him smile, I will say to Him: "My will is Yours and Yours is mine; therefore, form in me the Kingdom of your Divine Fiat."

Lesson of the Queen of Heaven to her child:

My dearest child, oh! how I long for you to be in my arms, to have the great contentment of being able to say to our little Baby King: "Do not cry, my pretty One. See, here with us is my little child, who wants to recognize You as King and give You dominion in her soul, to let You lay the Kingdom of your Will within her."

Now, child of my Heart, while you are all intent on longing for the little Child Jesus, pay attention and listen to Me. You must know that it was midnight when the little newborn King came out of my maternal womb. But the night turned into day; He who was the Lord of light put to flight the night of the human will, the night of sin, the night of all evils; and as the sign of what He was doing in the order of souls, with His usual Omnipotent Fiat the midnight turned into most refulgent daylight. All created things ran to sing praise to their Creator in that little Humanity. The sun ran to give its first kisses of light to little Baby Jesus, and to warm Him with its heat; the ruling wind, with its waves, purified the air of the stable, and with its sweet moaning said to Him: "I love You"; the heavens were shaken from their very foundations; the earth exulted and trembled down to the abyss; the sea roared with its gigantic waves. In sum, all created things recognized that their Creator was now in their midst, and they all competed in singing His praises. The very Angels, forming light in the air, with melodious voices which could be heard by all, said: "Glory to God in the highest, and peace on earth to men of good will. The Celestial

Baby is now born in the grotto of Bethlehem, wrapped in poor swaddling clothes..." - so much so, that the shepherds who were in vigil, listened to the angelic voices and ran to visit the little Divine King.

My dear child, continue to listen to Me. As I received Him into my arms and gave Him my first kiss, I felt the need of love to give something of my own to my Baby Son; and offering Him my breast, I gave Him abundant milk – milk formed in my person by the Divine Fiat Itself, in order to nourish little King Jesus. But who can tell you what I experienced in doing this; and the seas of grace, of love, of sanctity, that my Son gave to Me in return? Then I wrapped Him in poor but clean little clothes, and I placed Him in the manger. This was His Will, and I could not do without executing It. But before doing this, I shared Him with dear Saint Joseph, placing Him in his arms; and – oh! how he rejoiced. He pressed Him to his heart, and the sweet little Baby poured torrents of grace into his soul. Then, together with Saint Joseph, we arranged a little hay in the manger, and detaching Him from my maternal arms, I laid Him in it. And your Mother, enraptured by the beauty of the Divine Infant, remained kneeling before Him most of the time. I put all my seas of love into motion, which the Divine Will had formed in Me, to love Him, adore Him, and thank Him.

And what did the Celestial little Child do in the manger? A continuous act of the Will of our Celestial Father, which was also His; and emitting moans and sighs, He wailed, cried and called to everyone, saying in His loving moans: "Come all of you, children of mine; for love of you I am born to sorrow and to tears. Come all of you, to know the excess of my love. Give Me shelter in your hearts." And there was a coming and going of shepherds, who came to visit Him, and to all He gave His sweet gaze and His smile of love, amid His very tears.

Now, my child, a little word to you: you must know that all my joy was to hold my dear Son Jesus on my lap, but the Divine Will made Me understand that I should place Him in the manger, at everyone's disposal, so that whoever wanted to, could caress Him, kiss Him, and take Him in his arms, as if He were his own. He was the little King of all, therefore they had the right to make of Him a sweet pledge of love. And I, in order to fulfill the Supreme Volition, deprived Myself of my innocent joys, beginning, with works and sacrifices, the office of Mother, of giving Jesus to all.

My child, the Divine Will is demanding and wants everything, even the sacrifice of the holiest things; and according to the circumstances, the great sacrifice of depriving oneself of Jesus Himself; but this, in order to extend Its Kingdom even more, and to multiply the life of Jesus Himself. In fact, when the creature, out of love for Him, deprives herself of Him, her heroism and sacrifice is so great, as to have the virtue of producing a new life of Jesus, to be able to form another dwelling for Jesus.

Therefore, dear child, be attentive and, under any pretext, never deny anything to the Divine Will.

The soul:

Holy Mother, your beautiful lessons confound me; but if You want me to put them into practice, do not leave me alone, so that, when You see me succumb under the enormous weight of the divine privations, You may press me to your maternal Heart; and I will feel the strength never to deny anything to the Divine Will.

Little Sacrifice:

Today, to honor Me, you will come as many as three times to visit little Baby Jesus, and to kiss His tiny little hands; and you will say to Him five acts of love, to honor His tears and to calm His crying.

Ejaculatory Prayer:

Holy Mother, pour the tears of Jesus into my heart, that He may dispose in me the triumph of the Will of God.

Day Twenty-three[2]

**The Queen of Heaven in the Kingdom of
the Divine Will.
Here sounds the First Hour of Sorrow.
A Star, with mute Voice, calls the Magi to adore
Jesus. A Prophet makes himself the Revealer of the
Sorrows of the Sovereign Queen.**

The soul to her Queen Mother:

My most sweet Mother, here I am again at your knees;
this child of yours can no longer be without You, my
Mother. The sweet enchantment of the Celestial Baby,
whom You now clasp in your arms, and now adore on
your knees and love in the manger, enraptures me,
thinking that your happy destiny and the very little
King Jesus are nothing other than the fruits and the
sweet and precious pledges of that Fiat which extended
Its Kingdom in You. O please! oh! Mother, give me your
word that You will make use of your power to form in
me the Kingdom of the Divine Will.

Lesson of my Celestial Mother:

My dearest child, how happy I am to have you close to
Me, to be able to teach you how the Kingdom of the
Divine Will can extend in all things. All crosses,
sorrows, humiliations, invested by the life of the Divine
Fiat, are like raw materials in Its hands, in order to
nourish Its Kingdom and to extend It more and more.

Therefore, pay attention to Me, and listen to your Mother. I continued my stay in the grotto of Bethlehem with Jesus and dear Saint Joseph. How happy we were. Because of the presence of the Divine Infant and of the Divine Will operating in us, that little grotto had changed into Paradise. It is true that pains and tears were not lacking, but compared to the immense seas of joy, of happiness, of light, which the Divine Fiat made arise in each of our acts, they were just little drops plunged into these seas. And then, the sweet and lovable presence of my dear Son was one of my greatest happinesses.

Now, dear child, you must know that the eighth day arrived after the Celestial Baby had been born to the light of the day, and the Divine Fiat sounded the hour of sorrow, commanding us to circumcise the charming little Baby. It was a most painful cut which little Jesus was to undergo. It was the law of those times that all the firstborn had to undergo this painful cut. It can be called the law of sin, but my Son was innocent and His law was the law of love; but in spite of this, because He came to find, not the man-king, but the man degraded, in order to make Himself his brother and to elevate him, He wanted to lower Himself, and He submitted Himself to the law.

My child, Saint Joseph and I felt a shiver of pain, but intrepid and without hesitating, we called the minister and we had Him circumcised with a most painful cut. At the bitter pain, Baby Jesus cried and flung Himself into my arms, asking for my help. Saint Joseph and I mixed our tears with His; we gathered the first Blood shed by Jesus for love of creatures, and we gave Him the name of Jesus – powerful name, which was to make Heaven and earth tremble, and even hell; a name which was to be balm, defense, help for every heart.

Now, my child, this cut was the image of the cruel cut that man had done to his soul by doing his own will; and my dear Son allowed Himself to be given this cut in order to heal the harsh cut of the human wills, and, with His Blood, to heal the wounds of the many sins which the poison of the human will has produced in the creatures. So, each act of human will is a cut that is given, and a wound that opens; and the Celestial Baby, with His painful cut, prepared the remedy for all the human wounds.

Now, my child, another surprise: a new star shines under the vault of the heavens, and with its light, it goes in search of adorers, to lead them to recognize and adore Baby Jesus. Three individuals, each distant from the other, are struck by it, and invested by supreme light, they follow the star, which leads them to the grotto of Bethlehem, to the feet of Baby Jesus. What was not the astonishment of these Magi Kings, in recognizing in that Divine Infant the King of Heaven and earth – the One who had come to love and save all? In fact, in the act in which the Magi were adoring Him, enraptured by that celestial beauty, the newborn Baby made His Divinity shine forth from His little Humanity, and the grotto changed into Paradise; so much so, that they were no longer able to detach themselves from the feet of the Divine Infant – not until He again withdrew the light of the Divinity within His Humanity. And I, putting in exercise the office of Mother, spoke at length of the descent of the Word, and fortified them in faith, hope and charity, symbolized by their gifts offered to Jesus; and, full of joy, they withdrew into their regions, to be the first propagators.

My dear child, do not move from my side; follow Me everywhere. Forty days from the birth of little King Jesus are about to sound when the Divine Fiat calls us to the Temple in order to fulfill the law of the Presentation of my Son. So we went to the Temple. It was the first time that we went out together with my sweet Baby. A vein of sorrow opened in my Heart: I was going to offer Him as victim for the salvation of all. We entered the Temple, and first we adored the Divine Majesty; then we called the priest, and having placed Him in his arms, I made the offering of the Celestial Baby to the Eternal Father - offering Him in sacrifice for the salvation of all. The priest was Simeon, and as I placed Him in his arms, he recognized that He was the Divine Word and exulted with immense joy; and after the offering, assuming the attitude of prophet, he prophesied all my sorrows. Oh! how the Supreme Fiat sounded over my maternal Heart - thoroughly, with vibrating sound, the mournful tragedy of all the pains of my Baby Son. But what pierced Me the most were the words that the holy prophet spoke to Me: "This dear Baby will be the salvation and the ruin of many, and will be the target of contradictions."

If the Divine Will had not sustained Me, I would have died instantly of pure pain. But It gave Me life, and used it to form in Me the Kingdom of sorrows, within the Kingdom of Its very Will. So, in addition to the right of Mother which I had over all, I acquired the right of Mother and Queen of all Sorrows. Ah! yes, with my sorrows I acquired the little coin to pay the debts of my children, and also of the ungrateful children.

Now, my child, you must know that in the light of the Divine Will I already knew all the sorrows I was to suffer - and even more than that which the holy prophet told Me. But in that act, so solemn, of offering my Son, in hearing it being repeated to Me, I felt so pierced that my Heart bled, and deep gashes opened in my soul.

Now, listen to your Mother: in your pains, in the sorrowful encounters which are not lacking for you, never lose heart; but with heroic love let the Divine Will take Its royal place in your pains, that It may convert them for you into little coins of infinite value, with which you will be able to pay the debts of your brothers, to ransom them from the slavery of the human will, so as to make them enter again, as free children, into the Kingdom of the Divine Fiat.

The soul:

Holy Mother, in your pierced Heart do I place all my pains; and You know how they pierce my heart. O please! be my Mother, and pour into my heart the balm of your sorrows, that I may share in your same destiny of using my pains as little coins in order to conquer the Kingdom of the Divine Will.

Little Sacrifice:

Today, to honor Me, you will come into my arms, that I may pour in you the first Blood that the Celestial Baby shed in order to heal the wounds that your human will did to you; and you will recite three acts of love in order to mitigate the spasm of the wound of Baby Jesus.

Ejaculatory Prayer:

My Mother, pour your sorrow into my soul, and convert all my pains into Will of God.

Day Twenty-four

The Queen of Heaven in the Kingdom of the Divine Will.

A Cruel Tyrant. Little King Jesus is brought by His Mother and by Saint Joseph into a foreign Land, as Poor Exiled Ones. Return to Nazareth.

The soul to her Queen, overwhelmed by Sorrow:

My Sovereign Mother, your little child feels the need to come to your maternal knees to keep You a little company. I see your face veiled with sadness, and a few fleeting tears flowing from your eyes. The sweet little Baby is shivering, and, sobbing, He cries. Holy Mother, I unite my pains to yours in order to comfort You and to calm the crying of the Celestial Baby. But, O please! my Mother, do not refuse to reveal to me your secret. What is it that is so gloomy for my dear little Baby?

Lesson of the Mother Queen:

My dearest child, today the Heart of your Mother is swollen with love and with sorrow, so much so, that I cannot refrain from crying. You know of the coming of the Magi Kings, who caused rumor in Jerusalem, asking about the new King. And cruel Herod, for fear that his throne might be overthrown, has already given the mandate to kill my sweet Jesus, my dear Life, together with all the other children.

My child, what sorrow! The One who has come to give life to all, and to bring into the world the new era of peace, of happiness, of grace - they want to kill Him! What ingratitude, what perfidy! Ah! my child, to what extent the blindness of the human will reaches! To the extent of becoming ferocious, of tying the hands of the very Creator, and of making itself the master of the One who created it. Therefore, give Me your compassion, my child, and try to calm the crying of the sweet Baby. He cries because of the human ingratitude, because, only a newborn, they want Him dead; and in order to save Him, we are forced to flee. Dear Saint Joseph has already been told by the Angel to leave quickly for a foreign land. You - accompany us, dear child; do not leave us alone, and I will continue to give you my lessons on the grave evils of the human will.

Now, you must know that as soon as man withdrew from the Divine Will, he broke off with his Creator. Everything had been made by God on earth – everything was His; and man, by not doing the Divine Will, lost all rights, and it can be said that he had no place on which to put his foot. So, he became the poor exiled one, the pilgrim who could not posses a permanent room; and this, not only for the soul, but also for the body. All things became mutable for poor man; and if he has any fleeting thing, it was by virtue of the foreseen merits of this Celestial Baby. This, because the whole magnificence of Creation was destined by God for those who would do His Will and live in Its Kingdom. All others, if they manage to take anything, are the true petty thieves of their Creator; and with reason: they do not want to do the Divine Will, and want the goods that belong to It!

Now, dear child, listen to how much I and this dear Baby love you, for at the first dawn of His life He goes into exile, and into a foreign land, in order to free you from the exile in which your human will put you, so as to call you back to live, not in a foreign land, but in your Fatherland, which was given to you when you were created – that is, the Kingdom of the Supreme Fiat. Child of my Heart, have pity on the tears of your Mother, and on the tears of this sweet dear Baby, as We, crying, ask you never to do your will. But, come back, We pray you, We implore you, into the bosom of the Divine Will, which so much longs for you.

Now, dear child, in the midst of the sorrow for human ingratitude, and amid the immense joys and happinesses that the Divine Fiat gave Us, and the feast that all Creation made for the sweet Baby, the earth became green again and flowery under our steps, to give homage to its Creator. The sun fixed on Him, and singing His praises with its light, it felt honored to give Him its light and heat. The wind caressed Him; the birds, almost like clouds, alighted around Us, and with their trills and songs, made the most beautiful lullabies for the dear Baby, to calm His crying and favor His sleep. My child, since the Divine Will was in Us, We had power over everything.

So we arrived in Egypt, and after a long period of time, the Angel of the Lord told Saint Joseph that we should return to the house of Nazareth, because the cruel tyrant had died. So we repatriated to our native lands.

Now, Egypt symbolizes the human will – a land full of idols; and wherever the little Child Jesus passed, He knocked down these idols and cast them into hell. How many idols the human will possesses - idols of vainglory, of self-esteem and of passions that tyrannize the poor creature. Therefore, be attentive; listen to your Mother, as I would make any sacrifice never to let you do your will, and would lay down even my life to give you the great good of living always in the bosom of the Divine Will.

The soul:

Most sweet Mother, how much I thank You for making me comprehend the great evil of the human will. Therefore I pray You, for the sake of the sorrow You suffered in the exile of Egypt, to make my soul go out of the exile of my will, and to make me repatriate to the dear Fatherland of the Divine Will.

Little Sacrifice:

Today, to honor Me, you will offer your actions united with mine, in act of gratitude to the Holy Baby, praying Him to enter into the Egypt of your heart in order to change it all into Will of God.

Ejaculatory Prayer:

My Mother, enclose little Jesus in my heart, that He may reorder it all into Divine Will.

Day Twenty-five[3]

**The Queen of Heaven in the Kingdom of the Divine Will. Nazareth, Symbol and Reality of the Kingdom of the Divine Fiat. Hidden Life.
The Depository, Source and Perennial Channel.**

The soul to her Sovereign Queen:

Most sweet Mother, here I am again at your maternal knees, as I find You together with the little child Jesus; and caressing Him, You tell Him your love story, and Jesus tells You His. Oh! how beautiful it is to find Jesus and the Mother speaking to each other. And the ardor of their love is so great that they remain mute – enraptured: the Mother in the Son, and the Son in the Mother. Holy Mother, do not put me aside, but keep me with You, so that, in listening to what You say, I may learn to love You and to do always the Most Holy Will of God.

Lesson of the Queen of Heaven:

Dearest child, oh! how I longed for you in order to continue my lessons on the Kingdom which the Supreme Fiat extended ever more within Me.

Now, you must know that for your Mother, for dear and sweet Jesus, and for Saint Joseph, the little house of Nazareth was a Paradise. Being the Eternal Word, my dear Son possessed the Divine Will within Himself, of His own virtue; immense seas of light, of sanctity, of joys and of infinite beauty resided in that little Humanity. I possessed the Divine Will by grace; and even though I could not embrace immensity, as did beloved Jesus – because He was God and Man, and I was always His finite creature – yet, in spite of this, the Divine Fiat filled Me so much, having formed Its seas of light, of sanctity, of love, of beauties and of happinesses; and the light, the love and everything that a Divine Will can possess, which came out of Us, were so great that Saint Joseph remained eclipsed, inundated, and lived of our reflections.

Dear child, in this house of Nazareth, the Kingdom of the Divine Will was in full force. Every little act of ours – that is, working, starting the fire, preparing the food – were all animated by the Supreme Volition, and were formed on the solidity of the sanctity of pure love. Therefore, from the littlest to the greatest of our acts, immense joys, happinesses and beatitudes were unleashed. And we remained so inundated as to feel

121

ourselves as though under a pouring rain of new joys and indescribable contentments.

My child, you must know that the Divine Will possesses, by nature, the source of joys, and when It reigns in the creature It delights in giving, in each one of her acts, the new continuous act of Its joys and happinesses. Oh! how happy we were. Everything was peace, highest union, and each of us felt honored in obeying the other. My dear Son also competed in wanting to be commanded by Me and by dear Saint Joseph in the little jobs. Oh! how beautiful it was to see Him in the act of helping His foster father in the smith-work, or to see Him take food. But how many seas of grace did He let flow in those acts for the good of creatures?

Now, dear child, listen to Me: in this house of Nazareth, the Kingdom of the Divine Will was formed in your Mother and in the Humanity of my Son, to make of It a gift for the human family, when they would dispose themselves to receive the good of this Kingdom. But even though my Son was King and I was Queen, yet We were King and Queen without a people. Our Kingdom, though It could enclose all and give life to all, was deserted, because Redemption was needed first, in order to prepare and dispose man to come into this Kingdom so holy. More so, since It was possessed by Me and by my Son, who belonged to the human family according to the human order, as well as to the Divine Family by virtue of the Divine Fiat and of the Incarnate Word, and therefore creatures received the right to enter into this Kingdom. And the Divinity gave the right, and left the doors open to those who wanted to enter. So, our hidden life of so many years served to prepare the Kingdom of the Divine Will for creatures. And this is why I want to make known to you what this Supreme Fiat operated in Me, so that you may forget your will, and as you hold the hand of your Mother, I may lead you into the goods which, with so much love, I have prepared for you.

Tell Me, child of my Heart, will you make Me content, and also your and my dear Jesus, as We await you with so much love in this Kingdom so holy, to live together with Us, and to live only of Divine Will?

Now listen, dear child, to another trait of love which my dear Jesus made for Me in the house of Nazareth: He made of Me the depository of the whole of His life. When God does a work, He does not leave it suspended, or in the empty space, but He always looks for a creature in whom to be able to enclose and place the whole of His work. Otherwise, there would be the danger that God might expose His works to uselessness – which cannot be. Therefore, my dear Son placed in Me His works, His words, His pains – everything. He deposited even His breath into His Mother. And when, withdrawn in our little room, He would speak sweetly and narrate to Me all the Gospels He was to preach to the public, the Sacraments He was to institute, He entrusted everything to Me; and depositing everything in Me, He constituted Me perennial channel and source, because His life and all His goods were to come from Me for the good of all creatures. Oh! how rich and happy I felt in feeling that all that my dear Son Jesus did, was being deposited in Me. The Divine Will which reigned in Me gave Me the space to be able to receive everything, and Jesus felt the requital from His Mother of love and glory of the great work of Redemption. What did I not receive from God, because I never did my will, but always His? Everything; even the very life of my Son was at my disposal; and while it remained always in Me, I could bilocate it, to give it to whomever would ask Me for it with love.

Now, my child, a little word to you. If you do always the Divine Will and never your own, and you live in It, I, your Mother, will make the deposit of all the goods of my Son in your soul. Oh, how fortunate you will feel - you will have a divine life at your disposal, which will give you everything. And I, acting as your true Mother, will put Myself on guard, so that this life may grow in you, and form in you the Kingdom of the Divine Will.

The soul:

Holy Mother, I abandon myself into your arms. I am a little daughter who feels the extreme need of your maternal cares. O please! I pray You to take this will of mine and to enclose it in your Heart. Never give it to me again, that I may be happy to live always of Divine Will; and so I will make You and my dear Jesus content.

Little Sacrifice:

Today, to honor Me, you will come to make three little visits in the house of Nazareth to honor the Holy Family, reciting three Pater, Ave, Gloria, praying us to admit you to live in our midst.

Ejaculatory Prayer:

Jesus, Mary and Joseph, take me with you to live in the Kingdom of the Will of God.

Day Twenty-six

The Queen of Heaven in the Kingdom of the Divine Will. The Hour of Sorrow approaches. Painful Separation. Jesus in His Public and Apostolic Life.

The soul to her Celestial Mother:

Here I come again to You, my Queen Mother. Today, my love of daughter toward You makes me run to be spectator of when my sweet Jesus, separating from You, goes on His way to form His apostolic life in the midst of creatures. Holy Mother, I know that You will suffer very much; each moment of separation from Jesus will cost You your life; and I, your child, do not want to leave You alone. I want to dry your tears, and with my company, I want to break your loneliness; and as we remain together, You will continue to give me your beautiful lessons on the Divine Will.

Lesson of the Queen of Heaven:

My dearest child, your company will be very pleasing to Me, because in you I will feel the first gift that Jesus gives Me – a gift made of pure love, produced by His sacrifice and mine; a gift which will cost Me the life of my Son.

Now, pay attention to Me and listen. Hear, my child: a life of sorrow, of loneliness and of long separations from my Highest Good, Jesus, begins for your Mother. His hidden life is ended, and He feels the irresistible

126

need of love to go out in public, to make Himself known, and to go in search of man, lost in the maze of his will, and prey to all evils. Dear Saint Joseph had already died; Jesus was leaving, and I remained alone in the little house.

When my beloved Jesus asked Me for the obedience to leave – because He did nothing without first telling Me – I felt a blow in my Heart, but knowing that that was the Supreme Will, immediately I pronounced my Fiat - I did not hesitate one instant; and between my Fiat and the Fiat of my Son, We separated. In the ardor of our love, He blessed Me, and He left Me. I accompanied Him with my gaze while I could, and then, withdrawing, I abandoned Myself in that Divine Will which was my life. But – oh! power of the Divine Fiat - this Holy Will never let Me lose sight of my Son, nor did He lose Me; on the contrary, I felt His heartbeat in mine, and Jesus felt mine in His.

Dear child, I had received my Son from the Divine Will, and whatever this Holy Will gives, is not subject either to ending or to suffering separation - Its gifts are permanent and eternal. Therefore, my Son was mine; no one could take Him away from Me - neither death, nor sorrow, nor separation – because the Divine Will had given Him to Me. So, our separation was the appearance, but in reality We were fused together; more so, since one was the Will that animated Us. How could We separate?

Now, you must know that the light of the Divine Will allowed Me to see how badly and with how much ingratitude they treated my Son. He directed His step toward Jerusalem; His first visit was to the holy Temple, in which He began the series of His preachings. But - ah! sorrow - His word, full of life, bearer of peace, of love and of order, was misinterpreted and badly listened to - especially by the erudite and the learned of those times. And when my Son said that He was the Son of God, the Word of the Father, the One who had come to save them, they took such offense that they wanted to devour Him with their furious gazes. Oh, how my beloved Good, Jesus, suffered. His creative word, rejected, made Him feel the death which they gave to His divine word; and I was all attention, all eyes, in looking at that Divine Heart, bleeding, and I offered Him my maternal Heart to receive the same wounds, to console Him and give Him a support when He was about to succumb. Oh! how many times, after imparting His word, I saw Him forgotten by all, without anyone who would offer Him a refreshment; alone – alone, outside of the city walls; outside, under the vault of the starry heavens, leaning on a tree, crying and praying for the salvation of all. And I, your Mother, dear child, cried with Him from my little house; and in the light of the Divine Fiat, I sent Him my tears as refreshment, my chaste embraces and my kisses as comfort.

But in seeing Himself rejected by the great, the learned, my beloved Son did not stop, nor could He stop - His love ran, because He wanted souls. So He surrounded Himself with the poor, the afflicted, the sick, the lame, the blind, the mute, and with many other maladies by which the poor creatures were oppressed – all of them images of the many evils which the human will had produced in them. And dear Jesus healed everyone; He consoled and instructed everyone. So He became the friend, the father, the doctor, the teacher of the poor.

My child, it can be said that the poor shepherds were the ones who received Him with their visits at His birth, and the poor are those who follow Him in the last years of His life down here, unto His death. In fact, the poor, the ignorant, are more simple, less attached to their own judgment, and therefore they are more favored, more blessed, and preferred by my dear Son; so much so, that He chose poor fishermen as Apostles, as pillars of the future Church.

Now, dearest child, if I wanted to tell you what my Son and I did and suffered during these three years of His public life, I would be too long. What I recommend to you is that in everything you may do and suffer, your first and last act be the Divine Fiat. In the Fiat I separated from my Son, and the Fiat gave Me the strength to make the sacrifice. In the same way, you will find strength for everything, even in the pains that cost you your life, if you enclose everything in the Eternal Fiat. Therefore, give your word to your Mother, that you will let yourself be found always in the Divine

Will. In this way, you too will feel the inseparability from Me and from our Highest Good, Jesus.

The soul:

Most sweet Mother, how I compassionate You in seeing You suffer so much. O please, I pray You, pour your tears and those of Jesus into my soul, to reorder it and enclose it in the Divine Fiat.

Little Sacrifice:

Today, to honor Me, you will give Me all your pains as company to my loneliness, and in each pain you will place an "I love You" for Me and for your Jesus, to repair for those who do not want to listen to the teachings of Jesus.

Ejaculatory Prayer:

Divine Mother, may your word and that of Jesus descend into my heart and form in me the Kingdom of the Divine Will.

Day Twenty-seven

The Queen of Heaven in the Kingdom of the Divine Will. Here sounds the Hour of Sorrow. The Passion. A Deicide. The Crying of all Nature.

The soul to her Sorrowful Mother:

My dear Sorrowful Mother, today, more than ever, I feel the irresistible need to be close to You. No, I will not move from your side, to be spectator of your bitter sorrows and to ask You, as your child, for the grace to place in me your sorrows and those of your Son Jesus, and also His very death; so that His death and your sorrows may give me the grace to make my will die continually, and make rise again, upon it, the life of the Divine Will.

Lesson of the Queen of Sorrows:

Dearest child, do not deny Me your company in so much bitterness. The Divinity has already decreed the last day of my Son down here. An Apostle has already betrayed Him, giving Him up into the hands of the Jews, to make Him die. My dear Son, taken by excess of love and not wanting to leave His children, whom He came to search for upon earth with so much love, has already left Himself in the Sacrament of the Eucharist, so that whoever wants Him, may possess Him. So, the life of my Son is about to end, and He is about to take flight to His Celestial Fatherland.

Ah! dear child, the Divine Fiat gave Him to Me, and in the Divine Fiat I received Him; and now, in the same Fiat, I give Him back. My Heart is torn; immense seas of sorrows inundate Me; I feel life leaving Me because of the atrocious spasm. But nothing could I deny to the Divine Fiat; on the contrary, I felt disposed to sacrifice Him with my own hands, had It wanted it so. The strength of the Divine Will is omnipotent, and I felt such strength by virtue of It, that I would have contented Myself with dying rather than deny anything to the Divine Will.

Now, my child, listen to Me: my maternal Heart is drowned with pains; just thinking that my Son, my God, my Life, must die, is more than death for your Mother. Yet, I know I must live. What torment, what deep gashes form in my Heart, piercing It all the way through with sharp swords. Yet, dear child, I grieve in saying this, but I must say this to you: in these pains and deep gashes, and in the pains of my beloved Son, there was your soul - your human will. Since it would not let itself be dominated by the Will of God, We covered it with pains, We embalmed it, We fortified it with our pains, so that it would dispose itself to receive the life of the Divine Will. Ah! if the Divine Fiat had not sustained Me and continued Its course with infinite seas of light, of joy, of happiness, alongside the seas of my bitter sorrows, I would have died as many times for as many pains as my dear Son suffered. Oh! how tortured I felt, when He made Himself seen for the last time - pale, with a sadness of death on His face, and with trembling voice, as though wanting to burst into sobs, He told me:

"Good-bye Mother. Bless your Son, and give Me the obedience to die. My Divine Fiat and Yours made Me be conceived, and my Divine Fiat and Yours must make Me die. Hurry, Oh dear Mother, pronounce your Fiat, and tell Me: 'I bless You and I give You the obedience to die crucified. So does the Eternal Will want, and so I too want'."

My child, what a blow to my pierced Heart. Yet, I had to say it, because there were no forced pains in Us, but all voluntary. So We blessed each other, and exchanging that gaze which is not able to detach any more from the beloved, my dear Son, my sweet Life, departed; and I, your sorrowful Mother, stayed. But the eye of my soul never lost sight of Him. I followed Him into the Garden, in His terrible agony, and – oh! how my Heart bled in seeing Him abandoned by all, even by His most faithful and dear Apostles.

Dear child, the abandonment of dear ones is one of the greatest sorrows for a human heart in the stormy hours of life; especially for my Son, who had loved them so much and done so much good to them, and who was in the act of giving His life for the very ones who had just abandoned Him in the extreme hours of His life – even more, they had run away. What sorrow! What sorrow! And I, in seeing Him agonize and sweat Blood, agonized together with Him and sustained Him in my maternal arms. I was inseparable from my Son; His pains were reflected in my Heart, liquefied by sorrow and by love, and I felt them more than if they were my own. So I followed Him the whole night; there was not one pain or accusation they gave Him, which did not resound in my Heart. But, at the dawn of the morning, unable to endure any longer, accompanied by the disciple John, by Magdalene and other pious women, I wanted to follow Him step by step, also corporally, from one tribunal to another.

My dearest child, I heard the roaring of the lashes that fell upon the naked body of my Son; I heard the mockeries, the satanic laughter, and the blows they gave Him on His head when they crowned Him with thorns. I saw Him when Pilate showed Him to the people – disfigured and unrecognizable. I felt deafened by the "Crucify Him, Crucify Him!" I saw Him take the Cross upon His shoulders, exhausted, panting. And I, unable to refrain, hastened my step to give Him my last embrace and to dry His face, all wet with Blood. But - no! there was no pity for Us. The cruel soldiers pulled Him by the ropes and made Him fall. Dear child, what harrowing pain, not being able to help my dear Jesus in so many pains. Every pain opened a sea of sorrow in my pierced Heart. Finally, I followed Him to Calvary, where, amid unheard-of pains and horrible contortions, He was crucified and lifted up on the Cross. Only then was it conceded to Me to be at the foot of the Cross, to receive from His dying lips the gift of all my children, and the right and seal of my Maternity over all creatures. Shortly after, amid unheard-of spasms, He breathed His last.

All nature wore mourning, and cried over the death of its Creator. The sun cried, obscuring itself and withdrawing, horrified, from the face of the earth. The earth cried with a strong tremor, ripping open in various places, for the sorrow of the death of its Creator. All cried: the sepulchers by opening, the dead by rising; and even the veil of the Temple cried with sorrow by ripping open. All lost joy, and felt terror and fright. My child, your Mother remained petrified with sorrow, waiting to receive Him into my arms, to close Him in the sepulcher.

Now, listen to Me in my intense sorrow; with the pains of my Son I want to speak to you of the great evils of your human will. Look at Him in my sorrowful arms, how disfigured He is. He is the true portrait of the evils that the human will does to the poor creatures. My dear Son wanted to suffer so many pains in order to raise this will again - fallen into the abyss of all miseries; each pain of Jesus and each one of my sorrows called it to rise again in the Divine Will. Our love was so great that in order to place this human will in safety, We filled it with our pains, up to the point of drowning it and enclosing it inside the immense seas of my sorrows, and of those of my beloved Son.

Therefore, on this day of sorrows for your sorrowful Mother - and all for you - in return give Me your will, into my hands, that I may enclose it in the bleeding wounds of Jesus, as the most beautiful victory of His Passion and death, and as the triumph of my most bitter sorrows.

The soul:

Sorrowful Mother, your words wound my heart, and I feel myself dying in hearing that it was my rebellious will that made You suffer so much. Therefore I pray You to enclose it in the wounds of Jesus, that I may live of His pains and of your bitter sorrows.

Little Sacrifice:

Today, to honor Me, you will kiss the wounds of Jesus, saying five acts of love, and praying Me that my sorrows may seal your will in the opening of His sacred side.

Ejaculatory Prayer:

May the wounds of Jesus and the sorrows of my Mother give me the grace to make my will rise again in the Will of God.

Day Twenty-eight

The Queen of Heaven in the Kingdom of the Divine Will. Limbo. The Expectation. Victory over Death. The Resurrection.

The soul to her Mother Queen:

Pierced Mother, your little child, knowing that You are alone, without your beloved Good, Jesus, wants to remain clinging to You to keep You company in your most bitter desolation. Without Jesus, all things change into sorrow for You. The memory of His harrowing pains, the sweet sound of His voice which still resounds in your ear, the charming gaze of dear Jesus, now sweet, now sad, now swollen with tears, but which always enraptured your maternal Heart – as You don't have them with You any more, they are like sharp swords which pierce your pierced Heart through.

Desolate Mother, your dear child wants to give You relief, an act of compassion, for each pain. Even more, I would like to be Jesus, to be able to give You all the love, all the comforts, reliefs and compassion which Jesus Himself would have given You in this state of yours, of bitter desolation. Sweet Jesus gave me to You as your child; therefore, put me in His place in your maternal Heart, and I will be all of my Mother; I will dry your tears, and I will always keep You company.

Lesson of the Desolate Queen and Mother:

Dearest child, thank you for your company; but if you want your company to be sweet and dear to Me, and bearer of relief to my pierced Heart, I want to find in you the Divine Will operating and dominating, and that you do not surrender even one breath of life to your will. Then, yes, will I exchange you with my Son Jesus, because, His Will being in you, in It I will feel Jesus in your heart, and – oh, how happy I will be to find in you the first fruit of His pains and of His death. In finding my beloved Jesus in my child, my pains will change into joys, and my sorrows into conquests.

Now, listen to Me, child of my sorrows: as my dear Son breathed His last, He descended into Limbo, as triumpher and bearer of glory and happiness to that prison in which were all the Patriarchs and Prophets, the first father Adam, dear Saint Joseph, my holy parents, and all those who had been saved by virtue of the foreseen merits of the future Redeemer. I was inseparable from my Son, and not even death could take Him away from Me. So, in the ardor of my sorrows I followed Him into Limbo and was spectator of the feast, of the thanksgivings, which that whole great crowd of people gave to my Son, who had suffered so much, and whose first step had been toward them, to beatify them and to bring them with Himself to celestial glory. So, as He died, conquests and glory began for Jesus and for all those who loved Him. This, dear child, is symbol of how, as the creature makes her will die through union with the Divine Will, conquests of divine order, glory and joy begin, even in the midst of the greatest sorrows.

Even though the eyes of my soul followed my Son and I never lost sight of Him, at the same time, during those three days in which He was buried, I felt such yearnings to see Him risen, that in my ardor of love I kept repeating: "Rise, my Glory! Rise, my Life!" My desires were ardent, my sighs, of fire - to the point of feeling consumed.

Now, in these yearnings, I saw that my dear Son, accompanied by that great crowd of people, went out of Limbo in act of triumph, and brought Himself to the sepulcher. It was the dawn of the third day, and just as all nature had cried over Him, now it rejoiced; so much so, that the sun anticipated its course to be present at the act in which my Son was rising again. But – oh marvel - before rising again, He showed that crowd of people His Most Holy Humanity - bleeding, wounded, disfigured; the way it had been reduced for love of them and of all. All were moved, and admired the excesses of love and the great portent of Redemption.

Now, my child, oh, how I wish you to be present in the act in which my Son rose again. He was all Majesty; His Divinity, united to His soul, unleashed seas of light and of enchanting beauty, such as to fill Heaven and earth; and, as triumpher, making use of His power, He commanded His dead Humanity to receive His soul again, and to rise, triumphant and glorious, to immortal life. What a solemn act! My dear Jesus triumphed over death, saying: "Death, you will no longer be death - but life."

With this act of triumph, He placed the seal that He was Man and God; and with His Resurrection, He confirmed His doctrine, His miracles, the life of the Sacraments, and the whole life of the Church. Not only this, but He obtained triumph over the human wills, weakened and almost extinguished to true good, to make triumph over them the life of that Divine Will which was to bring to creatures the fullness of sanctity and of all goods. And at the same time, by virtue of His Resurrection, He cast into the bodies the seed of resurrection to everlasting glory. My child, the Resurrection of my Son encloses everything, says everything, confirms everything, and is the most solemn act that He did for love of creatures.

Now, listen to Me, my child; I want to speak to you as the Mother who loves her child very much. I want to tell you what it means to do the Divine Will and to live of It; and my Son and I give you the example. Our life was strewn with pains, with poverty, with humiliations, to the point of seeing my beloved Son dying of pains; but in all this ran the Divine Will. It was the life of our pains, and We felt triumphant and conquerors, to the extent of changing even death into life; so much so, that in seeing the great good, We voluntarily exposed ourselves to suffering because, since the Divine Will was in Us, no one could impose himself on It, or on Us. Suffering was in our power, and We called upon it as nourishment and triumph of Redemption, so as to be able to bring good to the entire world.

Now, dear child, if your life and your pains have the Divine Will as their center of life, be certain that sweet Jesus will use you and your pains to give help, light and grace to the whole universe. Therefore, pluck up courage; the Divine Will knows how to do great things wherever It reigns; and in all circumstances, reflect yourself in Me and in your sweet Jesus, and move forward.

The soul:

Holy Mother, if You help me and keep me sheltered under your mantle, acting as my celestial sentry, I am certain that I will convert all my pains into Will of God; and I will follow You, step by step, along the interminable ways of the Supreme Fiat, because I know that your charming love of Mother and your power will conquer my will, and You will keep it in your power and exchange it with the Divine Will. Therefore, my Mother, I entrust myself to You, and I abandon myself into your arms.

Little Sacrifice:

Today, to honor Me, you will say seven times: "Not my will, but Yours be done", offering Me my sorrows to ask Me for the grace that you may always do the Divine Will.

Ejaculatory Prayer:

My Mother, for the sake of the Resurrection of your Son, make me rise again in the Will of God.

Day Twenty-nine

The Queen of Heaven in the Kingdom of the Divine Will. The Hour of the Triumph. Apparitions of Jesus. The Fugitives cling around the Virgin as the Ark of Salvation and of Forgiveness. Jesus departs for Heaven.

The soul to her Mother Queen:

Admirable Mother, here I come to You again, on your maternal knees, to unite myself with You in the feast and triumph of the Resurrection of our dear Jesus. How beautiful is your appearance today – all loveliness, all sweetness, all joy. I seem to see You risen together with Jesus. O please, oh Holy Mother, in so much joy and triumph, do not forget your child. Rather, enclose the seed of the Resurrection of Jesus in my soul, so that, by virtue of It, I may rise again fully in the Divine Will, and live always united with You and with my sweet Jesus.

Lesson of the Queen of Heaven:

Blessed child of my maternal Heart, great was my joy and my triumph in the Resurrection of my Son; I felt reborn and risen again in Him. All my sorrows changed into joy and into seas of graces, of light, of love, of forgiveness for creatures, and laid my Maternity over all my children, given to Me by Jesus, with the seal of my sorrows.

Now listen to Me, dear child: you must know that after the death of my Son I withdrew in the cenacle, together with beloved John and Magdalene. But my Heart was pierced because only John was near Me, and in my sorrow I said: "And the other Apostles - where are they?"

But as they heard that Jesus had died, touched by special graces, all moved and weeping, one by one, the fugitives drew around Me, surrounding Me like a crown; and with tears and sighs, they asked for my forgiveness for they had so cravenly abandoned their Master, and had run away from Him. I welcomed them maternally in the ark of refuge and salvation of my Heart; I assured all of them of the forgiveness of my Son, and I encouraged them not to fear. I said to them that their destiny was in my hands, because He had given them all to Me as my children, and I recognized them as such.

Blessed child, you know that I was present at the Resurrection of my Son. But I did not say a word to anyone, waiting for Jesus Himself to manifest Himself as risen, glorious and triumphant. The first one to see Him risen was the fortunate Magdalene; then the pious women. And all came to Me telling Me that they had seen Jesus risen, that the sepulcher was empty; and I listened to all, and with an air of triumph I confirmed all in the faith in the Resurrection. By evening, almost all of the Apostles had seen Him, and all felt as though triumphant at having been the Apostles of Jesus. What change of scene, dear child - symbol of those who have first let themselves be dominated by the human will, represented by the Apostles who run away, abandoning their Master; and their fear and fright is such that they hide, and Peter reaches the point of denying Him. Oh! if they had been dominated by the Divine Will, they would never have run away from their Master, but, courageous and as triumphers, would never have departed from His side, and would have felt honored to lay down their lives to defend Him.

Now, dear child, my beloved Son Jesus remained on earth, risen, for forty days. Very often He appeared to the Apostles and disciples to confirm them in the faith and certainty of His Resurrection; and when He was not with the Apostles, He was with His Mother in the cenacle, surrounded by the souls who had come out of Limbo. But as the term of the forty days expired, beloved Jesus instructed the Apostles, and leaving His Mother as their guide and teacher, He promised us the descent of the Holy Spirit. Then, blessing us all, He departed, taking flight for the vault of the heavens, together with that great crowd of people who had come out of Limbo. All those who were there, and they were a great number, saw Him ascend; but as He went up high, a cloud of light removed Him from their sight.

Now, my child, your Mother followed Him into Heaven, and was present at the great feast of the Ascension. More so, since the Celestial Fatherland was not foreign to Me; and then, the feast of my Son, ascended into Heaven, would not have been complete without Me.

Now a little word to you, dearest child. Everything you have heard and admired has been nothing other than the power of the Divine Will operating in Me and in my Son. This is why I so much love to enclose in you the life of the Divine Will - and operating life - because everyone has It, but the majority of them keep It suffocated and to their service. And while It could operate prodigies of sanctity, of grace, and works worthy of Its power, It is forced by creatures to remain with folded arms, unable to carry out Its power. Therefore, be attentive, and let the Heaven of the Divine Will extend within you and operate, with Its power, whatever It wants and however It wants.

The soul:

Most Holy Mother, your beautiful lessons enrapture me, and – oh, how I wish and yearn for the operating life of the Divine Will in my soul. I too want to be the inseparable one from my Jesus and from You, my Mother. But to be sure of this, You must take on the commitment to keep my will enclosed in your maternal Heart; and even if You should see that it costs me much, You must never give it to me. Only in this way will I be certain; otherwise, it will always be words, but I will never do facts. Therefore, your child commends herself to You, and hopes for everything from You.

Little Sacrifice:

Today, to honor Me, you will make three genuflections in the act in which my Son ascended into Heaven, and you will pray Him to make you ascend in the Divine Will.

Ejaculatory Prayer:

My Mother, with your power, triumph in my soul, and make me be reborn in the Will of God.

Day Thirty

The Queen of Heaven in the Kingdom of the Divine Will. The Teacher of the Apostles, Central Place of the Nascent Church, and Boat of Refuge. The Descent of the Holy Spirit.

The soul to her Celestial Mother:

Here I come to You again, Sovereign of Heaven. I feel so drawn to You that I count the minutes, waiting for your Supreme Height to call me in order to give me the beautiful surprises of your maternal lessons. Your love of Mother enraptures me, and in knowing that You love me, my heart rejoices, and I feel all the confidence that my Mother will give me so much love, so much grace, as to form the sweet enchantment to my human will; in such a way that the Divine Will may extend Its seas of light within my soul, and place the seal of Its Fiat in all my acts. O please! O Holy Mother, never leave me alone again, and let the Holy Spirit descend into me, that He may burn away all that does not belong to the Divine Will.

Lesson of the Queen of Heaven:

My blessed child, your words echo in my Heart, and feeling wounded, I pour Myself into you with my seas of graces. Oh, how they run toward my child, to give you the life of the Divine Will. If you are faithful to Me, I will leave you no more; I will always be with you, to give you the food of the Divine Will in each one of your acts, words and heartbeats.

Now listen to Me, my child: our Highest Good, Jesus, has departed for Heaven and is now before His Celestial Father, pleading for His children and brothers, whom He has left upon earth. From the Celestial Fatherland, He looks at everyone - no one escapes Him; and His love is so great that He leaves His Mother on earth as comfort, help, instruction and company for His children and mine.

Now, you must know that as my Son departed for Heaven, I remained together with the Apostles in the cenacle, waiting for the Holy Spirit. They were all around Me, clinging to Me, and we prayed together; they did nothing without my advice. And when I began to speak to instruct them or to narrate some anecdotes about my Son which they did not know – as for example, the details of His birth, His baby tears, His loving traits, the incidents that happened in Egypt, the so many wonders of the hidden life in Nazareth – oh, how attentive they were in listening to Me. They were enraptured in hearing the so many surprises, the so many teachings that He had given Me, which were to serve for them. In fact, my Son had said little or nothing about Himself to the Apostles, reserving for Me the task of making known to them how much He had loved them, and the details which only His Mother knew. So, my child, I was in the midst of my Apostles more than the sun of the day. I was the anchor, the wheel, the boat in which they found refuge, to be safe and sheltered from every danger. Therefore, I can say that I delivered the nascent Church upon my maternal knees, and that my arms were the boat in which I led Her to a safe harbor, and I still lead Her.

Then the time came for the descent of the Holy Spirit, promised by my Son, in the cenacle. What a transformation, my child. As they were invested, they acquired new science, invincible strength, ardent love. A new life flowed within them, which rendered them intrepid and courageous, in such a way that they scattered throughout the whole world to make Redemption known, and to lay down their lives for their Master. I remained with beloved John, and was forced to leave Jerusalem, as the storm of persecution began.

My dearest child, you must know that I still continue my magisterium in the Church - there is nothing which does not descend from Me. I can say that I pour my own self out for love of my children, and I nourish them with my maternal milk. Now, during these times, I want to display a yet more special love by making known how my whole life was formed in the Kingdom of the Divine Will. Therefore I call you onto my knees, into my maternal arms, so that, forming a boat for you, you may be sure to live in the sea of the Divine Will. Greater grace I could not give you. O please! I pray you, make your Mother content - come to live in this Kingdom so holy. And when you see that your will would want to have some act of life, come and take refuge in the safe boat of my arms, saying to Me: "My Mother, my will wants to betray me, and I deliver it to You, that you may put the Divine Will in its place."

Oh, how happy I will be if I am able to say: "My child is all mine, because she lives of Divine Will." And I will make the Holy Spirit descend into your soul, that He may burn away from you all that is human; and by His refreshing breath, He may rule over you and confirm you in the Divine Will.

The soul:

Divine Teacher, today your little child feels her heart swollen, to the point of pouring myself out in crying, and wetting your maternal hands with my tears. A veil of sadness invades me, and I fear that I will not profit from your many teachings and from your many more than maternal cares. My Mother, help me, fortify my weakness, put to flight my fears; and I, abandoning myself in your arms, will be certain to live fully of the Divine Will.

Little Sacrifice:

Today, to honor Me, you will recite seven Glory Be's in honor of the Holy Spirit, praying to Me that His prodigies may be renewed over the whole Holy Church.

Ejaculatory Prayer:

Celestial Mother, pour fire and flames into my heart, that they may consume me, and burn away all that is not Will of God.

Day Thirty-one

The Queen of Heaven in the Kingdom of the Divine Will. Transit from Earth to Heaven. Happy Entrance. Heaven and Earth celebrate the New Comer.

The soul to her Glorious Queen:

My dear Celestial Mother, I am back again in your maternal arms, and in looking at You, I see that a sweet smile arises on your most pure lips. Today your attitude is all festive; it seems to me that You want to narrate to me and confide to your child something that will surprise me even more. Holy Mother, O please! I pray You, with your maternal hands, touch my mind, empty my heart, that I may comprehend your holy teachings and put them into practice.

Lesson of the Queen of Heaven:

Dearest child, today your Mother is in feast, because I want to speak to you of my departure from earth to Heaven, on the day in which I completed fulfilling the Divine Will on earth. In fact, there was not one breath, or heartbeat, or step in Me, in which the Divine Fiat did not have Its complete act; and this embellished Me, enriched Me, sanctified Me so much, that even the Angels remained enraptured.

Now, you must know that before departing for the Celestial Fatherland, I returned again to Jerusalem with my beloved John. It was the last time that I went past the earth in mortal flesh, and the whole Creation, as though realizing it, prostrated Itself around Me. Even the fish of the sea that I crossed, unto the tiniest little bird, wanted to be blessed by their Queen; and I blessed them all, and gave them my last good-bye. So I arrived in Jerusalem, and withdrawing into an apartment where John brought Me, I enclosed Myself in it never to go out again.

Now, blessed child, you must know that I began to feel within Me such a martyrdom of love, united to ardent yearnings to reach my Son in Heaven, as to feel consumed - to the point of feeling infirm with love; and I had intense deliriums and swoonings, all of love. In fact, I did not know illness or any slight indisposition; in my nature, conceived without sin and lived completely of Divine Will, the seed of natural evils was missing. If pains courted Me so much, they were all in the supernatural order, and these pains were triumphs and honors for your Celestial Mother, and gave Me the field so that my Maternity would not be sterile, but conqueror of many children. Do you see then, dear child, what it means to live of Divine Will? It means to lose the seed of natural evils, which produce, not honors and triumphs, but weaknesses, miseries and defeats.

Therefore, dearest child, listen to the last word of your Mother who is about to leave for Heaven. I would not depart content if I did not leave my child safe. Before departing, I want to make my testament to you, leaving you as dowry that same Divine Will which your Mother possesses, and which engraced Me so much, to the point of making of Me the Mother of the Word, Lady and Queen of the Heart of Jesus, and Mother and Queen of all.

Listen, dear child, this is the last day of the month consecrated to Me. I have spoken to you with great love of that which the Divine Will operated in Me, of the great good It can do, and of what it means to let oneself be dominated by It. I have also spoken to you of the grave evils of the human will. But do you think that it was only to make you a simple narration? No, no; when your Mother speaks, She wants to give. In the ardor of my love, in each word I spoke to you, I bound your soul to the Divine Fiat, and I prepared for you the dowry in which you might live rich, happy, and endowed with divine strength.

Now that I am about to leave, accept my testament; may your soul be the paper on which I write the attestation of the dowry that I give to you, with the gold pen of the Divine Will, and with the ink of the ardent love that consumes Me. Blessed child, assure Me that you will not do your will, ever again. Place your hand on my maternal Heart, and promise Me that you will enclose your will in my Heart, so that, not feeling it, you will not have any occasion to do it, and I will bring it with Me to Heaven, as triumph and victory of my child.

O please! dear child, listen to the last word of your Mother, dying of pure love; receive my last blessing as seal of the life of the Divine Will that I leave in you, which will form your heaven, your sun, your sea of love and of grace. In these last moments, your Celestial Mother wants to drown you with love, and pour Her own self out into you, provided that I obtain my intent of hearing your last word – that you will content yourself with dying, and will make any sacrifice, rather than give one act of life to your will. Say it to me, my child - say it to me.

The soul:

Holy Mother, in the ardor of my sorrow, I say it to You crying: if You see that I am about to do one act alone of my will, make me die; come Yourself to take my soul into your arms, and take me up there; and from the heart, I promise, I swear, never - never to do my will.

The Queen of Love:

Blessed child, how content I am. I could not decide to narrate to you my departure for Heaven if I did not leave my child safe on earth, endowed with Divine Will. But know that from Heaven I will not leave you - I will not leave you orphan; I will guide you in everything, and from your smallest need, up to the greatest – call

Me, and immediately I will come to you to act as your Mother.

Now, dear child, listen to Me. I was already infirm with love. The Divine Fiat, in order to console the Apostles, and also Myself, allowed almost in a prodigious way that all the Apostles, except one, would surround Me like a crown at the moment I was about to depart for Heaven. All felt a blow to their hearts, and cried bitterly. I consoled them all; I entrusted to them, in a special way, the nascent Holy Church, and I imparted my maternal blessing to all, leaving in their hearts, by virtue of it, the paternity of love toward souls. My dear Son did nothing but come and go from Heaven; He could no longer be without His Mother. And as I gave my last breath of pure love in the endlessness of the Divine Will, my Son received Me in His arms and took Me to Heaven, in the midst of the angelic choirs that sang praise to their Queen. I can say that Heaven emptied Itself to come to meet Me. All celebrated for Me, and in looking at Me, remained enraptured and said in chorus: "Who is She, who comes from the exile, all cleaving to Her Lord - all beautiful, all holy, with the scepter of Queen? Her greatness is such that the Heavens have lowered themselves to receive Her. No other creature has entered these celestial regions so adorned and striking - so powerful as to hold supremacy over everything."

Now, my child, do you want to know who She is - for whom the whole of Heaven sings praise and remains enraptured? I am She who never did Her own will. The

Divine Will abounded so much with Me as to extend heavens more beautiful, suns more refulgent, seas of beauty, of love, of sanctity, such that I could give light to all, love and sanctity to all, and enclose everything and everyone within my heaven. It was the work of the Divine Will operating in Me that had accomplished such a great prodigy; I was the only creature entering Heaven, who had done the Divine Will on earth as It is done in Heaven, and who had formed Its Kingdom in my soul. Now, in looking at Me, the whole Celestial Court was amazed, because as they looked at Me, they found me heaven; and returning to look at Me, they found me sun; and unable to remove their gaze from Me, looking at Me more deeply, they saw Me sea, and found in Me also the most clear earth of my humanity, with the most beautiful flowerings. And, enraptured, they exclaimed: "How beautiful She is! She has everything centralized within Herself - She lacks nothing. Among all the works of Her Creator, She is the only complete work of the whole Creation."

Now, blessed child, you must know that this was the first feast made in Heaven for the Divine Will, which had worked so many prodigies in Its creature. So, at my entrance into Heaven, the whole Celestial Court celebrated that which, beautiful and great, the Divine Fiat can operate in the creature. Since then, these feasts have never been repeated, and this is why your Mother loves so much that the Divine Will reign in souls in an absolute way: to give It the field in order to let It repeat Its great prodigies and Its marvelous feasts.

The soul:

Mother of love, Sovereign Empress, O please! from the Heaven in which You gloriously reign, turn your pitying gaze upon the earth and have pity on me. Oh, how I feel the need of my dear Mother. I feel life missing in me without You; everything vacillates without my Mother. Therefore, do not leave me halfway on my path, but continue to guide me until all things convert into Will of God for me, so that It may form Its life and Its Kingdom in me.

Little Sacrifice:

Today, to honor Me, you will recite three Glory Be's to the Most Holy Trinity, to thank Them in my name for the great glory They gave Me when I was assumed into Heaven; and you will pray Me to come to assist you at the moment of your death.

Ejaculatory Prayer:

Celestial Mother, enclose my will in your Heart, and leave the Sun of the Divine Will in my soul.

Offering of the human will to the Celestial Queen

Most sweet Mother, here I am, prostrate at the foot of your throne. I am your little child, I want to give You all my filial love, and as your child, I want to braid all the little sacrifices, the ejaculatory prayers, my promises to never do my will, which I have made many times during this month of graces. And forming a crown, I want to place it on your lap as attestation of love and thanksgiving for my Mother.

But this is not enough; I want You to take it in your hands as the sign that You accept my gift, and at the touch of your maternal fingers, convert it into many suns, for at least as many times as I have tried to do the Divine Will in my little acts.

Ah! yes, Mother Queen, your child wants to give You homages of light and of most refulgent suns. I know that You have many of these suns, but they are not the suns of your child; so I want to give You mine, to tell You that I love You, and to bind You to loving me. Holy Mother, You smile at me and, all goodness, You accept my gift; and I thank You from the heart. But I want to tell You many things; I want to enclose my pains, my fears, my weaknesses, my whole being in your maternal Heart, as the place of my refuge - I want to consecrate my will to You. O please! my Mother, accept it; make of it a triumph of grace, and a field on which the Divine Will may extend Its Kingdom. This will of mine, consecrated to You, will render us inseparable, and will keep us in continuous relations. The doors of Heaven will not be closed for me, because, as I have consecrated my will to You, You will give me Yours in exchange. So, either the Mother will come and stay with her child on earth, or the child will go to live with her Mother in Heaven. Oh! how happy I will be.

Listen, dearest Mother, in order to make the consecration of my will to You more solemn, I call the Sacrosanct Trinity, all the Angels, all the Saints, and before all I protest - and with an oath - to make the solemn consecration of my will to my Celestial Mother.

And now, Sovereign Queen, as the fulfillment, I ask for your holy blessing, for myself and for all. May your blessing be the celestial dew which descends upon sinners to convert them, and upon the afflicted to console them. May it descend upon the whole world and transform it in good; may it descend upon the purging souls and extinguish the fire that burns them. May your maternal blessing be pledge of salvation for all souls.

Appendix

The following six lessons and meditations were also written by Luisa at a later time, and were included in book "The Queen of Heaven in the Kingdom of the Divine Will" published in 1937 under the care of Luisa's confessor. They are being added here below as an appendix which enriches and expands the thirty one lessons of the "Virgin Mary in the Kingdom of the Divine Will".

Day Twenty (a)[4]

The Queen of Heaven in the Kingdom of the Divine Will.

In the Ardor of Her Love, feeling Herself the Mother of Jesus, Mary sets out in search of Hearts to be Sanctified. Visit to St. Elisabeth; Sanctification of John.

The soul to her Celestial Mother:

Celestial Mother, your poor child has extreme need of You. Since You are my Mother and the Mother of Jesus, I feel the right to be near You, to place myself at your side, and to follow your steps in order to model mine. O please! Holy Mother, give me your hand, and take me with You, that I may learn to behave well in the different actions of my life.

Lesson of the Queen of Heaven:

Blessed child, how sweet is your company to Me. In seeing that you want to follow Me in order to imitate Me, I feel refreshment for the flames of love that devour Me. Oh! yes, having you near Me, I will be able to teach you more easily how to live of Divine Will. While you follow Me, listen to Me.

As soon as I became Mother of Jesus and your Mother, my seas of love doubled, and unable to contain them all, I felt the need to pour them out, and to be the first bearer of Jesus to creatures, even at the cost of great

163

sacrifices. But, what am I saying – sacrifices? When one really loves, sacrifices and pains are refreshments; they are reliefs and outpourings of the love that one possesses. Oh! my child, if you do not experience the good of sacrifice, if you do not feel how it brings the most intimate joys, it is a sign that the divine love does not fill all your soul, and therefore that the Divine Will does not reign as Queen in you. It alone gives such strength to the soul as to render her invincible and capable of bearing any pain.

Place your hand upon your heart, and observe how many voids of love there may be in it. Reflect: that secret self-esteem, that becoming disturbed at every slightest adversity, those little attachments you feel to things and to people, that tiredness in good, that bother caused in you by that which is not to your liking, are equivalent to as many voids of love in your heart; voids which, like little fevers, deprive you of the strength and of the desire to be filled with Divine Will. Oh! how you too will feel the refreshing and conquering virtue in your sacrifices, if you fill these voids with love.

My child, give Me your hand now, and follow Me, because I will continue to give you my lessons.

So I departed from Nazareth, accompanied by Saint Joseph, facing a long journey, and crossing mountains to go visit Elisabeth in Judea, who, in her advanced age, had miraculously become a mother. I went to her, not to make her a simple visit, but because I burned with the desire to bring her Jesus. The fullness of grace, of love, of light that I felt within Me, pushed Me to bring, to multiply – to increase a hundredfold the life of my Son in creatures.

Yes, my child, the love of Mother which I had for all men, and for you in particular, was so great, that I felt the extreme need to give my dear Jesus to all, so that all might possess Him and love Him. The right of Mother, given to Me by the Fiat, enriched Me with such power as to multiply Jesus as many times as there are creatures who want to receive Him. This was the greatest miracle I could perform: to have Jesus ready to give to whomever desired Him. How happy I felt.

How I wish that you too, my child, in approaching people and in making visits, would always be the bearer of Jesus, capable of making Him known, and yearning to make Him loved.

After several days of travel, finally I arrived in Judea, and I hastened to the house of Elisabeth. She came to meet Me in feast. At the greeting I gave her, marvelous phenomena occurred. My little Jesus exulted in my womb, and fixing on little John in the womb of his mother with the rays of His Divinity, He sanctified him, gave him the use of reason, and made known to him that He was the Son of God. And John leaped so vigorously with love and with joy that Elisabeth felt shaken. She too, touched by the light of the Divinity of my Son, recognized that I had become the Mother of God; and in the emphasis of her love, trembling with gratitude, she exclaimed: "Whence comes to me so much honor, that the Mother of my Lord should come to me?"

I did not deny the highest mystery; rather, I humbly confirmed it. Praising God with the song of the Magnificat – sublime canticle, through which the Church continuously honors Me - I announced that the Lord had done great things in Me, His handmaid, and that because of this, all peoples would call Me blessed.

My child, I felt devoured with the desire to pour out the flames of love that consumed Me, and to reveal my secret to Elisabeth, who also longed for the Messiah to come upon earth. A secret is a need of the heart which, irresistibly, is revealed to persons who are capable of understanding each other.

Who can ever tell you how much good my visit brought to Elisabeth, to John, and to their whole household? Each one remained sanctified, filled with gladness, felt unusual joys, and comprehended things unheard-of. And John, in particular, received all the graces which were necessary for him, to prepare himself to be the precursor of my Son.

Dearest child, the Divine Will does great and unheard-of things wherever It reigns. If I worked many prodigies, it was because It had Its royal place in Me. If you let the Divine Will reign in your soul, you too will become the bearer of Jesus to creatures – you too will feel the irresistible need to give Him to all.

The soul:

Holy Mother, how I thank You for your beautiful lessons. I feel that they have such power over me as to make me yearn continuously to live in the Divine Will. But so that I may obtain this grace – come, descend into my soul together with Jesus; renew for me the visit you made to St. Elisabeth and the prodigies You worked for her. Ah! yes, my Mother, bring me Jesus - sanctify me. With Jesus I will be able to do His Most Holy Will.

Little Sacrifice:

To honor Me, you will recite the Magnificat three times, in thanksgiving for the visit I made to St.

Elisabeth.

Ejaculatory Prayer:

Holy Mother, visit my soul, and prepare in it a worthy dwelling for the Divine Will.

Day Twenty-three (a)[5]

The Queen of Heaven in the Kingdom of the Divine Will. Here sounds the First Hour of Sorrow. Heroism in submitting the Infant Jesus to the Harsh Cut of Circumcision.

The soul to her Celestial Mother:

Divine Mother, your love calls me powerfully to You, because You want to let me share in your joys and in your sorrows, to enclose them in my heart as pledge of your love and of that of little Baby Jesus, that I may comprehend how much You have loved me, and how obliged I am to imitate You, keeping the model of your lives to make a perfect copy of them. And You, holy Mother, help me, that I may be able to imitate You.

Lesson of the Queen of Heaven:

Dearest child, how I long for your company, to tell you our story of love and of sorrow. Company renders joys more sweet, tender and dear, and sorrow is mitigated and compensated by the company of the one who loves us.

Now, you must know that only eight days had passed from the birth of the Divine Infant. Everything was feast and happiness; the very Creation, taking a festive attitude, celebrated the Baby Creator. But duty interrupted our joys, because in those times there was a law that all firstborn sons were to undergo the harsh cut of circumcision. My Heart of Mother bled with sorrow in having to submit my dear Son, my Life, my own Creator, to such a bitter pain. Oh! how I would have wanted to take His place. But the Supreme Volition imposed Itself on my love, and giving Me heroism, commanded Me to circumcise the Child God. My child, you cannot comprehend how much it cost Me; but the Divine Fiat won, and I obeyed, united with Saint Joseph. In mutual agreement, we had my dear Son circumcised. At the painful cut, I felt my Heart being torn, and I cried. Saint Joseph cried, and my dear Baby sobbed, and His pain was such that He shivered, and looking at me, He sought help in Me. What an hour of pain and of spasm for the three of us. It was such that, more than sea, it engulfed all creatures, to bring to them the first pledge and the very life of my Son, in order to place them in safety.

Now, blessed child, you must know that this cut enclosed profound mysteries: first, it was the seal that impressed in the little Humanity of the Celestial Baby His brotherhood with the whole human family; and the Blood that He shed was the first disbursement before Divine Justice in order to ransom all human generations. The dear Baby was innocent, He was not obliged to the law; but He wanted to submit Himself - first, to give the example; and then, to infuse trust, courage, and say to all: "Do not fear; I am a little brother of yours, similar to you. Let us love one another, and I will place you all in safety; I will bring you all to my Celestial Father, as my dear brothers."

My child, what an example the Celestial Baby gives: He, who is the Author of the law, obeys the law. He is born only eight days ago, and He makes it a duty for Himself, and submits Himself to the harsh cut of circumcision; an indelible cut - as indelible as the union He came to form with degraded humanity. This says that sanctity is in doing one's own duty, in the observance of the laws, and in fulfilling the Divine Will. Sanctity without duty does not exist. It is duty that places order, harmony, and the seal on sanctity.

Furthermore, my child, you must know that as Adam withdrew from the Divine Will, after his brief life of innocence, his human will remained wounded, more than by a deadly knife, and through this wound entered sin and passions. He lost the beautiful day of the Divine Will, and degraded himself so much as to arouse pity. And my dear Son, after the joys of His birth, wanted to be circumcised, so that this, His wound, might heal the wound that Adam did to himself by doing his own will; and with His Blood, He prepared for him the bath to wash him of all his sins, to fortify Him, to embellish him, in such a way as to render him worthy to receive again that Divine Will he had rejected, which formed his sanctity and his happiness. Child, there was not one work or pain that He suffered, which did not seek to reorder again the Divine Will in the creatures. Therefore, in all circumstances, even painful and humiliating, may you take to heart doing the Divine Will in everything, because they are the raw material in which It hides in order to operate in the creature, so as to let her acquire Its Life acting in the creature.

Now, dearest child, in so much sorrow, the most beautiful joy arises, such as to stop our tears. As He was circumcised, we gave Him the Most Holy Name of Jesus, wanted by the Angel. In pronouncing this Most Holy Name, the joy, the contentment, was such as to sweeten our sorrow. More so, since in this Name, whoever wanted to, would find balm for his pains, the defense in dangers, the victory in temptations, the hand so as not to fall into sin, the medicine for all his evils. This Most Holy Name of Jesus makes hell tremble; the Angels revere It, and It sounds sweet to the ear of the Celestial Father. Before this Name, all bow down and adore. Powerful Name, holy Name, great Name; whoever invokes It with faith will feel the marvels, the miraculous secret of the virtue of this Most Holy Name.

Now, my child, I recommend to you: pronounce this Name, "Jesus", always. When you see that your human will, weak, vacillating, hesitates in doing the Divine, the Name of Jesus will make it rise again for you in the Divine Fiat. If you are oppressed, call upon Jesus; if you work, call upon Jesus; if you sleep, call upon Jesus; and when you wake up, may your first word be "Jesus". Call Him always; it is a Name that contains seas of grace, but which He gives to those who call Him and love Him.

The soul to her Queen:

Celestial Mother, how I must thank You for the beautiful lessons You have given me. O please! I pray You, inscribe them in my heart, that I may never forget them. And I pray You to give the bath of the Blood of the Celestial Baby to my soul, that It may heal the wounds of my human will to enclose in them the Divine; and I pray You to write over each wound, as guard, the Most Holy Name of Jesus.

Little Sacrifice:

Today, to honor Me, you will do five acts of love to the Most Holy Name of Jesus, and will compassionate Me in the sorrow I suffered in the circumcision of my Son Jesus.

Ejaculatory Prayer:

My Mother, write "Jesus" inside my heart, that He may give me the grace to live of Divine Will.

Day Twenty-three (b)[6]

The Queen of Heaven in the Kingdom of the Divine Will. She leaves Bethlehem. The Divine Fiat calls Her to the Heroic Sacrifice of offering Baby Jesus for the Salvation of Mankind. The Purification.

The soul to her Celestial Mother:

Holy Mother, here I am close to You, to accompany You to the Temple, where You go to make the greatest of sacrifices – to place the life of the Celestial Infant at the mercy of each creature, that they may use it to reach safety and to be sanctified. But, ah! sorrow – many will use it to offend Him, and even to become lost. O please! my Mother, place little Jesus in my heart, and I promise You, I swear, to love Him always, and to keep Him as the life of my poor heart.

Lesson of the Queen of Heaven:

Dearest child, how happy I am to have you close to Me. My maternal Heart feels the need to pour out my love and to confide to you my secrets. Be attentive to my lessons, and listen to Me. You must know that for forty days now, we have been in this grotto of Bethlehem, the first home of my Son down here; but, how many wonders in this grotto! The Celestial Infant, in an ardor of love, descended from Heaven to earth; He was conceived, was born, and felt the need to pour out this love; so, each breath, heartbeat and motion, was an outpouring of love that He made. Each tear, wail and moan, was an outpouring of love. Even His feeling numb with cold, His tiny little lips, livid and shivering – were all outpourings of love that He made; and He looked for His Mother in whom to deposit this love, which He could no longer contain; and I was prey to His love. So, I felt Myself being wounded continuously, and I felt my dear little One palpitating, breathing, moving within my maternal Heart. I felt Him crying, moaning and wailing, and I remained inundated by the flames of His love. The circumcision had already opened deep gashes in Me, into which He poured so much love that I felt Queen and Mother of love. I felt enraptured in seeing that in each pain, tear and motion that my sweet Jesus made, He looked for and called upon His Mother, as dear refuge of His acts and of His life. Who can tell you, my child, what passed between Me and the Celestial Baby during these forty days? The repetition of His acts together with Me, His tears, His pains, His love, were as though transfused together, and whatever He did, I did.

Now, after the completion of the forty days, the dear Baby, drowned more than ever in His love, wanted to obey the law and present Himself to the Temple to offer Himself for the salvation of each one. It was the Divine Will that called us to the great sacrifice, and we promptly obeyed. My child, this Divine Fiat, when It finds promptness in doing what It wants, places at the creature's disposal Its divine strength, Its sanctity, Its creative power to multiply that act, that sacrifice, for all and for each one. In that sacrifice It places the little coin of infinite value, with which one can pay and satisfy for all. It was the first time that your Mother and Saint Joseph went out together with the little Child Jesus. All Creation recognized Its Creator, and felt honored at having Him in their midst; and assuming the attitude of feast, they accompanied us along the way. As we arrived at the Temple, we prostrated ourselves and adored the Supreme Majesty; and then we placed Him in the arms of the priest, who was Simeon, who made of Him an offering to the Eternal Father - offering Him for the salvation of all. And while he offered Him, inspired by God, he recognized the Divine Word, and exulting with immense joy, he adored and thanked the dear Baby. After the offering, he assumed the attitude of prophet, and predicted all my sorrows. Oh! how the Supreme Fiat, painfully, made my maternal Heart feel, with vibrating sound, the mournful tragedy of all the pains which my Divine Son was to suffer. Each word was a sharp sword that pierced Me. But what pierced my Heart the most was to hear that this Celestial Infant would be not only the salvation, but also the ruin of many, and the target of contradictions. What pain! What sorrow! If the Divine Will had not sustained Me, I would have died instantly of pure pain. But It gave Me life, to begin to form in Me the Kingdom of Sorrows within the Kingdom of Its very Divine Will. So, with the right of Mother which I had over all, I acquired also the right of Mother and Queen of all Sorrows. Oh! yes, with my sorrows, I acquired the little coin with which to pay the debts of my children, and also those of the ungrateful children.

Now, my child, you must know that through the light of the Divine Will that reigned in Me, I already knew all the sorrows I was to suffer - and even more than those which the holy prophet told me. Rather, I can say that he prophesied to Me the sorrows which were to come to Me from the outside, but he said not a word about my interior pains which would pierce Me more, and the interior pains between Me and my Son. But in spite of this, in that act, so solemn, of the offering of my Son, in hearing them being repeated to Me, I felt so pierced that my Heart bled, and new veins of sorrow and deep gashes opened in my soul.

Now, listen to your Mother: in your pains, in the sorrowful encounters which are not lacking for you either, when you know that the Divine Will wants some sacrifice of you - be ready, do not lose heart, but rather, repeat quickly the dear and sweet Fiat – that is: "Whatever You want, I want". And with heroic love, let the Divine Will take Its royal place in your pains, that It may convert them for you into the little coin of infinite value, with which you will be able to pay your debts, and also those of your brothers, to ransom them from the slavery of the human will, so as to make them enter, as free children, into the Kingdom of the Divine Fiat. In fact, you must know that the Divine Will is so pleased by the sacrifice wanted by It from the creature, that It gives her Its divine rights, and constitutes her queen of the sacrifice and of the good that will arise in the midst of creatures.

The soul to her Celestial Mother:

Holy Mother, in your pierced Heart I place all my pains; and You know how much they afflict me. O please! be my Mother, and pour the balm of your sorrows into my heart, that I may share your same destiny of using my pains as the cortege of Jesus, to keep Him defended and sheltered from all offenses, and as the sure means to conquer the Kingdom of the Divine Will, and make It come to reign upon earth.

Little Sacrifice:

Today, to honor Me, you will come into my arms, that I may offer you, together with my Son, to the Celestial Father, in order to obtain the Kingdom of the Divine Will.

Ejaculatory Prayer:

Holy Mother, pour your sorrow into my soul, and convert all my pains into Will of God.

Day Twenty-three (c)[7]

**The Queen of Heaven in the Kingdom of the Divine
Will. A New Star, with Its Sweet Twinkling, calls
the Magi to adore Jesus. The Epiphany.**

The soul to her Celestial Mother:

Here I am again, Holy Mother, on your maternal knees.
The sweet Baby whom You hold to your breast and
your enrapturing beauty bind me in such a way that I
cannot move away from You. But today your
appearance is even more beautiful. It seems to me that
the sorrow of the circumcision has rendered You more
beautiful. Your sweet gaze looks far away to see
whether people dear to You are coming, because You
feel the yearning of wanting to make Jesus known. I will
not move from your knees, so that I too may listen to
your beautiful lessons, and may come to know Him and
love Him more.

Lesson of the Queen of Heaven:

Dearest child, you are right in saying that you see Me as
more beautiful. You must know that when I saw my Son
circumcised and His Blood pouring from His wound, I
loved that Blood, that wound, and I became Mother
twice: Mother of my Son, and Mother of His Blood and
of His crude pain. So, I acquired a double right of
Maternity before the Divinity - a double right of graces

for Myself and for all mankind. This is why you see Me as more beautiful.

My child, how beautiful it is to do good, to suffer in peace for love of the One who created us. This binds the Divinity to the creature, and gives her so much, of graces and of love, to the point of drowning her. This love and these graces do not know how to remain idle, but want to run and give themselves to all, to make known the One who has given so much. This is why I felt the need to make my Son known.

Now, my blessed child, the Divinity, which can deny nothing to one who loves It, makes a new star, more beautiful and luminous, arise under the azure heavens; and with its light, it goes in search of adorers, to say to the whole world, with its mute twinkling: "The One who has come to save you is born. Come to adore Him and to know Him as your Savior."

But - human ingratitude! - among many, only three individuals paid attention, and heedless of the sacrifices, put themselves on the way to follow the star. And just as a star guided their persons along the journey, so did my prayers, my love, my yearnings, my graces – for I wanted to make known the Celestial Baby, the Awaited One from all centuries - descend into their hearts like many stars, illumine their minds, guide their interiors, in such a way that, without yet knowing Him, they felt that they loved the One whom they were looking for, and they hastened their steps in order to reach and see Him, whom they so much loved.

My dearest child, my Heart of Mother rejoiced at the faithfulness, correspondence and sacrifice of these Magi Kings, to come to know and adore my Son. But I cannot hide from you a secret sorrow of mine: among many, only three. And in the history of the centuries, how many times is this sorrow of mine and this human ingratitude not repeated! My Son and I do nothing but make stars arise, one more beautiful than the other, to call some to know their Creator, some to sanctity, some to rise again from sin, some to the heroism of a sacrifice. But do you want to know what these stars are? A sorrowful encounter is a star; a truth that one comes to know is a star; a love unrequited by other creatures is a star; a setback, a pain, a disillusion, an unexpected fortune, are as many stars that shed light in the minds of creatures. And caressing them, they want to make them find the Celestial Infant, who fidgets with love, and shivering with cold, wants a refuge in their hearts to make Himself known and loved. But, alas, I who hold Him in my arms, wait in vain for the stars to bring Me creatures, in order to place Him in their hearts, and my Maternity is constrained, hindered. And while I am the Mother of Jesus, I am prevented from being the Mother of all, because they are not around Me, they do not look for Jesus; the stars hide, and they remain in the Jerusalems of the world, without Jesus. What sorrow, my child, what sorrow! It takes correspondence, faithfulness, sacrifice, to follow the stars; and if the Sun of the Divine Will rises in the soul – how much attention does it not take. Otherwise, one remains in the darkness of the human will.

Now, my child, as the holy Magi Kings entered Jerusalem, they lost the star, but in spite of this they did not stop looking for Jesus. However, as they went outside the city, the star reappeared and led them, festive, into the grotto of Bethlehem. I received them with love of Mother, and the dear Baby looked at them with great love and majesty, letting His Divinity shine forth from His little Humanity. And so, bowing down, they knelt at His feet, adoring and contemplating that celestial beauty; they recognized Him as true God, and remained enraptured, ecstatic, while enjoying Him; so much so, that the Celestial Baby had to withdraw His Divinity into His Humanity, otherwise they would have remained there, without being able to move from His divine feet.

Then, as they came round from their rapture, in which they offered the gold of their souls, the incense of their belief and adoration, the myrrh of their whole beings and of any sacrifice He might want of them, they added the external offering and gifts, symbol of their interior acts: gold, incense and myrrh. But my love of Mother was not yet content; I wanted to place the sweet Baby in their arms, and – oh! with how much love they kissed Him and pressed Him to their breasts. They felt paradise in advance within them. With this, my Son bound all the gentile nations to the knowledge of the true God, and placed the goods of Redemption, the return to faith of all peoples, in common for all. He constituted Himself King of the rulers; and with the weapons of His love, of His pains and of His tears, ruling over everything, He called the Kingdom of His Will upon earth. And I, your Mother, wanted to be the first Apostle. I instructed them, I told them the story of my Son - His ardent love; I recommended that they make Him known to all, and taking the first place of Mother and Queen of all the Apostles, I blessed them, I had them blessed by the dear Baby, and, happy and in tears, they departed again for their regions. I did not leave them; I accompanied them with maternal affection, and to repay them, I let them feel Jesus in their hearts. How happy they were! You must know that only when I see that my Son has the dominion, the possession, and forms His perennial dwelling in the hearts that search for Him and love Him – then do I feel a true Mother.

Now a little word to you, my child: if you want Me to act as your true Mother, let me place Jesus in your heart. You will make Him happy with your love; you will nourish Him with the food of His Will, because He takes no other food; You will clothe Him with the sanctity of your works. And I will come into your heart, I will raise my dear Son again together with you, and will perform the office of Mother for you and for Him; in this way I will feel the pure joys of my maternal fecundity. You must know that anything which does not begin from Jesus, who is inside the heart – be they even the most beautiful external works – can never please Me, because they are empty of the life of my dear Son.

The soul to her Celestial Mother:

Holy Mother, how I must thank You for wanting to place the Celestial Baby into my heart - how happy I am. O please! I pray You to hide me under your mantle, that I may see nothing but the Baby who is inside my heart; and forming of all my being one single act of love of Divine Will, I may make Him grow so much, to the point of filling myself completely with Jesus, and nothing may be left of me but the veil that hides Him.

Little Sacrifice:

Today, to honor Me, you will come three times to kiss the Celestial little One, giving Him the gold of your will, the incense of your adorations, the myrrh of your pains; and you will pray Me to enclose Him in your heart.

Ejaculatory Prayer:

Celestial Mother, enclose me within the wall of the Divine Will, that I may nourish my dear Jesus.

Day Twenty-five (a)[8]

The Queen of Heaven in the Kingdom of the Divine Will. Visit to the Temple. Mary, Model of Prayer. Loss of Jesus. Joys and Sorrows.

The soul to her Celestial Mother:

Holy Mother, your maternal love calls me to You with ever more powerful voice. I see You now all busy, ready to leave Nazareth. My Mother, do not leave me, take me with You, and I will listen attentively to the rest of your sublime lessons.

Lesson of the Queen of Heaven:

Beloved child, your company and the care you show in listening to my celestial lessons in order to imitate Me are the purest joys you can procure for my maternal Heart. I delight because I am able to share with you the immense riches of my inheritance. Turning your gaze now to Jesus, now to Me, pay attention to Me; I will narrate to you an episode of my life which, though it had a consoling outcome, was yet most painful to Me. Imagine that if the Divine Will had not given Me continuous and new sips of strength and of grace, I would have died of pure spasm.

We continued to spend our lives in the quiet little house of Nazareth, and my dear Son grew in grace and in wisdom. He was charming because of the sweetness and the gentleness of His voice, the sweet enchantment

184

of His eyes, the loveliness of His whole person. Yes, my Son was truly beautiful, immensely beautiful!

He had recently reached the age of twelve, when we went to Jerusalem according to custom, in order to solemnize the Passover. We set out on the journey – He, Saint Joseph and I. Very often, as we proceeded, devout and recollected, my Jesus would break the silence and speak to us now of His Celestial Father, now of the immense love for souls which He felt in His Heart.

Once in Jerusalem, we went directly to the Temple, and as we arrived, we prostrated ourselves with our faces to the ground, we adored God profoundly, and prayed for a long time. Our prayer was so fervent and recollected as to open the Heavens, draw and bind the Celestial Father, and therefore hasten the reconciliation between Him and men.

Now, my child, I want to confide to you a pain that tortures Me. Unfortunately, there are many who go to church to pray, but the prayer that they direct to God remains on their lips, because their hearts and minds flee far away from Him. How many go to church out of pure habit, or to spend time uselessly. They close Heaven, instead of opening It. And how numerous are the irreverences committed in the house of God! How many scourges would be spared in the world, and how many chastisements would convert into graces, if all souls strived to imitate our example.

Only the prayer that springs from a soul in whom the Divine Will reigns, acts in an irresistible way over the Heart of God. It is so powerful as to conquer Him, and to obtain the greatest graces from Him. Therefore, take care to live in the Divine Will, and your Mother, who loves you, will give to your prayer the rights of Her powerful intercession.

After we had fulfilled our duty in the Temple and celebrated the Passover, we prepared to return to Nazareth. In the confusion of the crowd, we were separated; I remained with the women, and Joseph joined the men. I looked around to see whether my dear Jesus had come with Me, but not seeing Him, I thought He had remained with his father Joseph. But what was not the surprise and the consternation I felt when, as we arrived at the place at which we were to reunite, I did not see Him at his side. Unaware of what had happened, we felt such fright and such pain that we both remained mute. Overcome with sorrow, we went back hurriedly, anxiously asking those whom we met: "O please! tell us if you have seen Jesus, our Son, for we cannot live without Him." And, crying, we would describe His features: "He is all lovable; His beautiful azure eyes sparkle with light and speak to the heart; His gaze strikes, enraptures, enchains; His forehead is majestic; His face is beautiful, of an enchanting beauty; His most sweet voice descends deep into the heart and sweetens all bitternesses; His hair, curly and like finest gold, renders Him striking and charming. All is majesty, dignity, sanctity in Him. He is the most beautiful among the sons of men."

But in spite of all our searching, nobody was able to tell us anything. The sorrow I felt became so sharp as to make Me cry bitterly, and to open, at each instant, deep gashes in my soul, which caused Me true spasms of death.

Dear child, if Jesus was my Son, He was also my God; therefore my sorrow was all in the divine order – that is, so powerful and immense as to surpass all other possible torments together. If the Fiat which I possessed had not sustained Me continuously with Its divine strength, I would have died of dismay.

Seeing that no one was able to give us news, I anxiously questioned the Angels who surrounded Me: "But, tell Me, where is my beloved Jesus? Where should I direct my steps in order to find Him? Ah! Tell Him I can endure no more; bring Him to Me - into my arms, upon your wings. O please! my Angels, have pity on my tears, help Me - bring Me Jesus."

In the meantime, as every search had turned out in vain, we returned to Jerusalem. After three days of most bitter sighs, of tears, of anxieties and fears, we entered the Temple. I was all eyes and looked everywhere, when, finally, as though overcome with jubilation, I saw my Son in the midst of the doctors of the law. He was speaking with such wisdom and majesty as to make those who were listening remain enraptured and amazed. Upon merely seeing Him, I felt life come back to Me, and immediately I comprehended the secret reason of His being lost.

And now, a little word to you, dearest child. In this mystery, my Son wanted to give to Me and to you, a sublime teaching. Could you perhaps assume that He was ignoring what I was suffering? On the contrary, my tears, my searching, and my sharp and intense sorrow, resounded in His Heart. Yet, during those hours, so painful, He sacrificed to the Divine Will His own Mother, the one whom He loves so much, in order to show Me how I too, one day, was to sacrifice His very Life to the Supreme Will.

In this unspeakable pain, I did not forget you, my beloved one. Thinking that it would serve as an example for you, I kept it at your disposal, so that you too, at the appropriate time, might have the strength to sacrifice everything to the Divine Will. As Jesus finished speaking, we approached Him reverently, and addressed Him with a sweet reproach: "Son, why have You done this to us?" And He, with divine dignity, answered us: "Why were you looking for Me? Did you not know that I have come into the world to glorify my Father?" Having comprehended the high meaning of such answer, and adored in it the Divine Will, we returned to Nazareth.

Child of my maternal Heart, listen: when I lost my Jesus, the pain I felt was so very intense; yet, a second one added to this – that of your own being lost. In fact, in foreseeing that you would go far from the Divine Will, I felt deprived at once of the Son and of the daughter, and therefore my Maternity suffered a double blow.

My child, when you are in the act of doing your will rather than that of God, think that by abandoning the Divine Fiat, you are about to lose Jesus and Me, and to fall into the kingdom of miseries and of vices. Keep, then, your word, which you gave Me – to remain indissolubly united to Me – and I will grant you the grace to never again let yourself be dominated by your will, but exclusively by the Divine.

The soul:

Holy Mother, I tremble in thinking of the abysses into which my will is capable of making me fall. Because of it, I can lose You, I can lose Jesus, and all the celestial goods. Mother, if You do not help me, if You do not surround me with the power of the light of the Divine Will, I feel it is not possible for me to live of Divine Will with constancy. Therefore I place all my hope in You, in You I trust, from You I hope for everything. Amen.

Little Sacrifice:

You will recite three Hail Marys to compassionate the intense sorrow I felt during the three days in which I remained without my Jesus.

Ejaculatory Prayer:

Holy Mother, let me lose my will forever, to live only in the Divine Will.

Day twenty-five (b)[9]

The Queen of Heaven in the Kingdom of the Divine Will.
Queen of Families, Queen of Miracles.
Bond of Marriage between the Fiat and the Creature. The Wedding of Cana.

The soul to her Celestial Mother:

Holy Mother, here I am together with You and with sweet Jesus, to be present at a new wedding, to see its prodigies and comprehend its great mystery, and the extent of your maternal love for me and for all. O please! Mother of mine, take my hand in yours, place me on your knees, invest me with your love, purify my intelligence, and tell me why You wanted to be present at this wedding.

Lesson of the Queen of Heaven:

My dearest child, my Heart is swollen with love, and I felt the need to tell you the reason why, together with my Son Jesus, I wanted to be present at this wedding of Cana. Do you think it was because of a simple ceremony? No, child, there are profound mysteries. Pay attention to Me, and I will tell you new things, and how my love of Mother was displayed in an incredible manner, and the love of my Son gave true signs of paternity and royalty toward creatures.

Now listen to Me: my Son had come back from the desert, and was preparing Himself for His public life; but first He wanted to be present at this wedding, and therefore He allowed Himself to be invited. We went there, not to celebrate, but to work great things for the good of the human generations. My Son took the place of Father and King in the families, and I took the place of Mother and Queen. With Our presence We renewed the sanctity, the beauty, the order of the marriage formed by God in the Garden of Eden – that of Adam and Eve – married by the Supreme Being in order to populate the earth, and to multiply and increase the future generations. Marriage is the substance from which the life of the generations arises; it can be called the trunk from which the earth is populated. The priests, the religious, are the branches; but if it were not for the trunk, not even the branches would have life. Therefore, through sin, by withdrawing from the Divine Will, Adam and Eve caused the family to lose sanctity, beauty and order. And I, your Mother, the new innocent Eve, together with my Son, went to reorder that which God did in Eden; I constituted Myself Queen of families, and impetrated the grace that the Divine Fiat might reign in them, to have families that would belong to Me, and I might hold the place of Queen in their midst.

But this is not all, my child. Our love was burning, and We wanted to make known to them how much We loved them, and to give them the most sublime of lessons. And here is how: at the height of the lunch, wine lacked, and my Heart of Mother felt consumed with love, wanting to give help; and knowing that my

Son can do anything, with supplicating accents, but certain that He would listen to Me, I say to Him: "My Son, the spouses have no more wine." And He answers Me: "My hour to do miracles has not yet come." And knowing that He certainly would not deny to Me what His Mother asked of Him, I say to those who are serving the table: "Do whatever my Son tells you, and you will have what you want; even more, you will receive in addition, and in superabundance."

My child, in these few words I gave a lesson, the most useful, necessary and sublime for creatures. I spoke with the Heart of Mother and I said: "My children, do you want to be holy? Do the Will of my Son. Do not move from what He tells you, and you will have His likeness, His sanctity in your power. Do you want all evils to cease? Do whatever my Son tells you. Do you want any grace, even difficult? Do whatever He tells you and wants. Do you also want the necessary things of natural life? Do whatever my Son tells you; because in His words, in everything He tells you and wants, He encloses such power that, as He speaks, His word contains what you ask for, and makes the graces that you want arise within your souls. How many see themselves as full of passions, weak, afflicted, misfortuned, miserable; yet, they pray and pray, but because they do not do what my Son tells, they obtain nothing; Heaven seems to be closed for them. This is a sorrow for your Mother, because I see that while they pray, they move away from the source in which all goods reside – the Will of my Son.

Now, those who were serving did precisely what my Son told them – that is: "Fill the jars with water and bring them to the table." My dear Jesus blessed that water and it turned into delicious wine. Oh! a thousand times blessed, the one who does what He tells and wants! With this, my Son gave Me the greatest honor, He constituted Me Queen of miracles; this is why He wanted my union and my prayer in doing His first miracle. He loved Me too much - so much that He wanted to give Me the first place of Queen also in miracles. And with facts, not with words, He said: "If you want graces, miracles, come to my Mother; I will never deny Her anything She wants."

In addition to this, my child, with my presence at this wedding, I looked at the future centuries, I saw the Kingdom of the Divine Will upon earth, I looked at families, and I impetrated for them that they might symbolize the love of the Sacrosanct Trinity, so that Its Kingdom might be in full force. And with my rights of Mother and Queen, I took to heart Its regime; and possessing the source of it, I placed at the creatures' disposal all the graces, the helps, the sanctity, which are needed to live in a Kingdom so holy. And so I keep repeating: "Do whatever my Son tells you."

My child, listen to Me: look for nothing else, if you want to have everything in your power, and give Me the contentment of being able to make of you my true child, and child of the Divine Will. Then will I take on the commitment of forming the marriage between you and the Fiat; and acting as your true Mother, I will bind the marriage by giving you the very Life of my Son as dowry, and my Maternity and all my virtues as gift.

The soul:

Celestial Mother, how much I must thank You for the great love You have for me, and because, in everything You do, You always have a thought for me, and You prepare for me and give me such graces, that Heaven and earth are moved and enraptured together with me; and we all say: "Thank you! Thank you!" O please! Holy Mother, engrave within my heart your holy words: "Do whatever my Son tells you", so as to generate in me the life of the Divine Will, which I so much long for and desire. And You, seal my will, that it may always be submitted to the Divine.

Little Sacrifice:

In all our actions, let us prick up our ears to listen to our Celestial Mother, who says to us: "Do whatever my Son tells you", that we may do everything in order to fulfill the Divine Will.

Ejaculatory Prayer:

Holy Mother, come into my soul, and do for me the miracle of making me possessed by the Divine Will.

---

[1] See also Appendix: Day Twenty (a).

[2] See also Appendix: Day Twenty-three (a), Day Twenty-three (b) and Day Twenty-three (c).

[3] See also Appendix: Day Twenty-five (a) and Twenty-five (b).

[4] This lesson corresponds to the 17th meditation of the book "The Queen of Heaven in the Kingdom of the DivineWill." As the original was not found, this lesson has been taken from that book. It can be placed between Day Twenty and Day Twenty-one.

[5] This lesson is original from Luisa, taken from a separate handwritten notebook. It expands the lesson of Day 23.

[6] This lesson is original from Luisa, taken from a separate handwritten notebook. It expands the lesson of Day 23.

[7] This lesson is original from Luisa, taken from a separate handwritten notebook. It expands the lesson of Day 23.

[8] This is the 24th meditation of the book "The Queen of Heaven in the Kingdom of the Divine Will". As the original was not found, this lesson has been taken from that book.

[9] This is the 25th meditation of the book "The Queen of Heaven in the Kingdom of the Divine Will", but here it is according to the original from Luisa, taken from a separate handwritten notebook.

Milton Keynes UK
Ingram Content Group UK Ltd.
UKHW020855100924
1572UKWH00051B/489